Kirstin von Gl...

111 Gardens
in London
That You
Shouldn't Miss

© Emons Verlag GmbH
All rights reserved
© Photographs: Kirstin von Glasow, except:
Brown Hart Gardens (ch. 10): mauritius images/Greg Balfour Evans/Alamy
© Cover motif: shutterstock.com/VMM and shutterstock.com/Maria Stezhko
Design: Eva Kraskes, based on a design
by Lübbeke | Naumann | Thoben
Maps: altancicek.design, www.altancicek.de
Edited by Alison Jean Lester
Printing and binding: Hitzegrad Print Medien & Service –
Lensing Druck Gruppe, Feldbachacker 16, 44149 Dortmund
Printed in Germany 2017
ISBN 978-3-7408-0143-4
First edition

Did you enjoy it? Do you want more?
Join us in uncovering new places around the world on:
www.111places.com

Foreword

London covers roughly 580 square miles, and 47 per cent of it is green spaces, including 3,000 parks, 30,000 allotments, three million gardens and two national nature reserves. As a result, I had no difficulty in finding enough material for this book. The problem was to choose between so many amazing gardens, each with its own individual character and beauty.

The Royal Parks such as Hyde Park, Regent's Park and Kensington Gardens with their wealth of history, landscaped and ornamental gardens had to be included. Then there were the council parks, created in the 19th century in response to the demand for green spaces in overcrowded urban districts. These parks often have great sport facilities and a more relaxed planting style.

The garden squares bear testimony to a whole different tradition. They were created for the private use of the residents of a housing development. The city grew around large green spaces that are remnants of country estates or ancient forests. Examples are Hampstead Heath or Highgate Wood. Other exciting green spaces run along old railway lines (Parkland Walk), canals (Regent's Canal) or small rivers (Wandle Trail). There are big (Richmond Park) and small (Camley Street Natural Park), nature reserves and many beautiful community gardens, which are the perfect places to observe the British passion for gardening. Volunteers are the heart and soul of these gardens, but none of the big parks could manage without them either.

Don't forget to visit the roof garden, City Farms and the 'magnificent' garden cemeteries. If you are still on your feet and eager to see more, explore the hundreds of private gardens open every year for charity in London under the National Open Garden Scheme (www.ngs.org.uk) or during Open Square Weekend (www.opensquares.org).

The gardens portrayed in this book are my personal choice but you can go out and find your own favourite gardens and hopefully enjoy yourself as much as I did making this book!

111 Gardens

1 Alexandra Palace Park

Victorian views

Lovingly known as Ally Pally, the Victorian entertainment venue Alexandra Palace and its park is famous for its year-round indoor ice rink. But there's so much more to the park, starting with its lively past.

Created by landscape architect Alexander McKenzie, the park opened its gates in 1863. At its highest point sits Alexandra Palace, which first opened in 1873 as a northern counterpart to the hugely successful Crystal Palace about 14 miles due south. First named The People's Palace, it was re-christened Alexandra Palace after the popular Princess of Wales. Disaster struck when it burned down only 16 days after its inauguration, but it was re-opened two years later.

While the palace hosted many exciting events over the following years and became the birthplace of the BBC, the park also had its share of excitement such as the building of an airship in its grounds, parades and horse races.

The racecourse closed in 1970, but the park remains a true 'people's park'. There's a cricket ground, a pitch and putt course, a football field, a soft play adventure playground and a skate park. Tree-climbing courses can be booked; visitors who'd rather move on the ground can go on a segway rally. The floating dragons on the boating lake are for hire and immensely popular with kids! Most Sundays a large farmers market near the Muswell Hill entrance sells local produce, international food and handmade preserves, cakes and biscuits. Two cafés and a pub offer a variety of food options. 'Plantaholics' can get excited about the recently planted orchard and wander through the old oaks, chestnuts and rare snake's head fritillary in the wilder areas of the park, or just sit on a bench in the rose garden and enjoy the views over London. Apropos of views: It is worth going once around Ally Pally to appreciate the panoramic view over different parts of North London!

Address Alexandra Palace Way, N22 7AY, www.alexandrapalace.com, feedback@alexandrapalace.com | Getting there Tube to Wood Green (Piccadilly Line); bus W3; or train to Alexandra Palace (Great Northern) | Hours Unrestricted | Tip Check out the CUFOS Community Centre in the former Alexandra Palace Railway Station. It offers adult classes and plenty of activities for children.

2 All Hallows Church Garden

A beautiful Southwark bombsite

At the time when All Hallows Church was built in 1879 by George Gilbert Scott Jr, the area was described as 'one of the most poverty stricken woe begotten and heathenish spots in Southwark'. Today it seems more romantic than woe begotten. The garden on Copperfield Street – also known as Copperfield Street Community Garden – is located opposite the quaint Winchester Cottages, built by the ecclesiastical commissioners under the influence of social reformer Octavia Hill from 1893-1895.

During World War II bombs destroyed the church, and today All Hallows is one of the last undeveloped bombsites in Central London. In 1957 the church was replaced by a smaller chapel, incorporating parts of the original building. The community garden was born when this church was closed in 1971. It lies along the aisle of the old church and has a perimeter brick wall on the side of the street. Two stone arches remain from All Hallows and a crucifix was installed on the former church altar. The garden was laid out with a central lawn surrounded by flowerbeds and benches. There is also a small sunken area and the walls are covered with decades-old ivy, a favourite nesting site for wrens, robins and blackbirds. Bats and squirrels are also frequent visitors. It is a tranquil place and everyone who comes across it stops to take it in.

Since its beginning the garden has been looked after entirely by local volunteers. They were disappointed when the owner of the site, Southwark Cathedral, wanted to develop the plot and build flats for private rent. The volunteers who manage the garden fought for its preservation as a community space that is open to all. After many protests, Southwark Cathedral withdrew the planning application and the garden remains in the hands of local volunteers, supported by Bankside Open Spaces Trust. That doesn't mean it isn't heavenly, though!

Address Copperfield Street, SE1 0EP, www.saveallhallows.com | Getting there Tube to Borough (Northern Line) | Hours Unrestricted | Tip The Copperfield Gallery in the repurposed church hall exhibits interesting contemporary artists (www.copperfieldgallery.com).

3 Archbishop's Park

Nature's most beautiful gift

Tucked behind Lambeth Palace, this nearly 10-acre park doesn't surprise visitors with elaborate bedding schemes or glamorous perennial borders. It is a real neighbourhood hub and ideal to visit with small children who will enjoy the pirate ship on the playground. They run around here freely because the park is completely cut off from the street. The sports facilities include football pitches, cricket nets and tennis courts that underwent a major upgrade in 2016. There is also the bower, a wooden shelter carved by local craftsman Arthur de Mowbray with a roof made of red cedar and seats carved from a single oak. Some say it looks like an armadillo, others see a woodlouse. Whatever it is, it looks pretty impressive from afar.

The more you explore the park, the more beautiful little details you discover. There is a little wildlife pond and a wildflower meadow as well as several insect hotels. A community orchard was planted in 2010. From autumn to early spring, pink cyclamen flower beneath the trees. Small mosaics made by Southbank Mosaics can be found all over the park. One of them depicts a tree of life and was made with the help of local children and the Archbishop of Canterbury. The Friends of Archbishop's Park are behind most of these loving details. They also founded several gardening clubs that support adults recovering from mental health issues.

A social agenda also motivated the founding of the park. Archbishop Tait (1811–1882) donated nine acres of Lambeth Palace Gardens to the 'local poor'. Trees were planted, a playground, lawn and sports fields were laid out and it was opened to the public in 1901. Since then this green space has become a gift to many people in the area. A quote from Albert Einstein that is carved into a tree trunk in the park hits the nail on the head: 'Joy in looking and comprehending is nature's most beautiful gift.'

Address Carlisle Lane, SE1 7LE, www.lambeth.gov.uk/places/archbishops-park, friendsofarchbishopspark@gmail.com | Getting there Tube to Lambeth North (Bakerloo Line) | Hours 7.30am–15 minutes before sunset | Tip The adjacent Lambeth Palace Garden is worth a visit but opens only once a month to the public (www.archbishopofcanterbury.org).

4 Arnold Circus

A wedding cake for the poor

This unique garden lies at the centre of the Boundary Estate, arguably the world's first council estate. This area of Bethnal Green, known as the 'Old Nichol', had been one of the worst slums in London from 1830 onwards. The *Illustrated London News* described it in 1863: 'It is but one painful and monotonous round of vice, filth and poverty, huddled in dark cellars, ruined garrets, bare and blackened rooms, reeking with disease and death, and without the means, even if there were the inclination, for the most ordinary observations of decency or cleanliness.' Following the initiative of the local Reverend Osborne Jay, and Arthur Morrison's fictionalised description in *A Child of the Jago*, the slum was demolished and a new estate built. The earth dug out for the red brick housing blocks was used to create the raised garden of the circus – officially 'Boundary Gardens' – and its wedding-cake appearance was achieved by terracing the garden and topping it with a bandstand.

But the attractive new tenements were deemed too beautiful for the 'undeserving poor' that lived here before. Only 11 were granted a flat. The rest went to the 'industrious' poor, including policemen, nurses and teachers.

In the late 20th century the circus fell into disrepair but the Friends of Arnold Circus initiated a major refurbishment in 2010, repairing the bandstand, refurbishing the railings and installing seating. An underground rainwater harvesting system delivers water for watering the revived garden. There's something in flower all year round, from bluebells, bleeding heart, and daffodils in spring, hollyhocks, meadow-rue and cranesbills as well as wildflower patches in summer to hellebores and snowdrops in winter. Once again the circus is the centre of an active community, and although the area has become increasingly gentrified, residents' groups have fought to keep two-thirds of the flats in the hands of Tower Hamlets Borough Council.

Address Arnold Circus, E2 7JR, www.arnoldcircus.co.uk, contact@foac.org.uk | Getting there London Overground to Shoreditch High Street (East London Line) | Hours Unrestricted | Tip Visit the unique Boundary Community Launderette, run by Boundary Estate residents for over 20 years (28 Calvert Avenue).

5__Arnos Park

Crufts in Enfield

London spread rapidly in the late 19th and early 20th century. Areas formerly belonging to large estates were broken up and suburban houses were built. This only became possible because the public transport system was enlarged and improved. Arnos Park in the London borough of Enfield is the result of both developments.

For a long time the Walker family resisted selling any part of their Arnos Grove Estate. Instead, they created three miles of pleasure walks in the 300-acre grounds. In 1918, the shipping magnate Lord Inverforth bought the estate and broke it up for development. A parcel of 44.5 acres was purchased by Southgate Urban District Council and became Arnos Park in 1928. Public transport arrived here in 1933 in the form of an impressive, 34-arch brick viaduct. It carries the Piccadilly Line and from afar trains can be seen rushing across it.

Visitors enter the park from Morton Crescent through ornamental iron gates and cross a pretty green wooden bridge. The park consists mainly of grassland with some wooded areas with ancient oaks and hornbeam trees. A large variety of birds can be spotted regularly, including great spotted woodpeckers, pied wagtails, chaffinches and siskins nesting here in winter. One of the most charming sights is Pymmes Brook, a tributary to the River Lea, meandering through the grounds, lined by weeping willows. A small waterfall murmurs steadily.

The park also comprises a bowling green, tennis courts, a children's playground and a recently planted orchard in the community gardens. What's more, the very active residents group, Friends of Arnos Park, not only mobilises locals to clean up the park, maintain the flower beds and prune trees; every September they organise Canine Capers, a dog show where the 'happiest dog', 'best disguised dog' and 'fastest dog in in The North (of London)' are crowned. Who says life in suburbia isn't fun?

Address Arnos Grove, Walker Close, N11 1AQ, www.friendsofarnospark.wordpress.com, friendsofarnospark@hotmail.co.uk | **Getting there** Tube to Arnos Grove (Piccadilly Line) | **Hours** Mon–Fri 8am–dusk; Sun 8.30am–dusk | **Tip** The Pymmes Brook Walking Trail follows Pymmes Brook through various North London Parks (10 miles) and ends at Pickett's Lock in Enfield.

6__Barbican

Concrete lily pads

You either hate the Barbican or you love it! Either way it is worth seeing the lake and gardens in the centre of this Brutalist landmark. The Le Corbusier-influenced architects Chamberlin, Powell and Bon built the complex between 1963 and 1976. The rising concrete tower blocks house flats, an arts centre, restaurants and cafés. Arranged around a central lake, they remind one of a castle (the name Barbican comes from the Latin *barbicana,* meaning fortified tower) and visible remnants of medieval walls are incorporated in the structure. A maze of Venetian-inspired covered high walks leads you around the estate, offering various views of the lake and gardens. At the eastern end of the lake, water cascades down a concrete structure. A sunken garden takes the form of giant water lily pads planted with reeds, grasses, geraniums, climbers – and of course water lilies can also be found in abundance!

The newly planted Beech Gardens is a roof garden in the north-west of the estate, created by Nigel Dunnett, who is also responsible for the planting at the Queen Elizabeth Olympic Park. This low-maintenance garden has a colourful planting scheme, where one or two flowering plants take centre stage at a time. Altogether 22,000 herbaceous plants were used but there are only a few trees, such as black alder or viburnum.

The Fann Street Wildlife Garden is another of the gardens on the estate. This garden with wildflower meadow, cottage garden, pond and herb garden is managed by residents and open to the public only on Open Garden Squares Weekend. Last but not least there is the wonderful Barbican Conservatory with its exotic trees and plants. Little wooden bridges lead to small ponds populated by terrapins and exotic fish. On Sundays you can have afternoon tea here.

Whether you hate or love the Brutalist architecture, the gardens are always worth a visit!

Address Silk Street, EC2Y 8DS, www.barbican.org.uk, tickets@barbican.org.uk | Getting there Tube to Barbican (Circle, Hammersmith & City and Metropolitan Lines) | Hours Sun noon–5pm (conservatory) | Tip Visit one of the many performances, plays or concerts at the Barbican Centre!

7 _ Battersea Park

Peace Pagoda and dog riots

Where do you find a walk fit for apes, a riot-inducing dog and a monk beating a drum at dawn? Insiders will recognise Battersea Park immediately. All others can look forward to exploring its many exciting features.

Once a popular duelling ground, the 205–acre park consists of flat marshland. It was created between 1846 and 1864 by James Pennethorne, who also designed Victoria Park in East London. A large lake with rocks and cascades was finished in 1870, complete with Italianate pump house to supply water for the cascades (now home to a contemporary art gallery). The Sub-Tropical Gardens, laid out in 1863 by John Gibson, were the first such public gardens in Britain.

Another crucial event in the park's history was the 1951 Festival of Britain when Battersea Park hosted the Festival Pleasure Gardens containing fairground rides, a shopping area, flower gardens and children's areas. In 2004 these neglected gardens were restored and re-named the Russell Page Gardens after the landscape architect who designed them.

There is also the restored Rose Garden, the Thrive Garden – a therapeutic garden to support people with disabilities, and the new Winter Garden that comes into its own when nothing else flowers. A winding path north of the English Garden takes visitors to a sculpture of a dog, erected in 1985 to replace an earlier, destroyed one commemorating a terrier said to have been insufficiently anaesthetised during a vivisection at University College in 1903. Medical students and anti-vivisectionists fought over the issue in the 'Brown Dog Riots'. Another attraction erected in 1985 is the Peace Pagoda, maintained by Reverend Gyoro Nagase, a Buddhist monk who usually can be seen at dawn walking to the pagoda, gently beating a drum.

And if all this is just too serene, go ape at Go Ape, which offers vertigo-inducing tree-top walks in the southwest corner of the park!

Address Between Albert Bridge Road and Chelsea Bridge Road, SW11 4NJ, www.batterseapark.org | Getting there London Overground to Battersea Park (South London Line) | Hours Daily 6.30am–10.30pm | Tip If you've got little ones in tow, visit the children's zoo!

8 __ Bonnington Square Garden
Two for one

At the entrance of Bonnington Square Garden the visitor is greeted by the sculpture of a large open hand balancing on top of a pergola. The 'helping hand' is a fitting introduction to this small but very lush garden grown out of the engagement of the local community. A nine-metre industrial wheel, rescued from a marble factory, has now nearly vanished behind plants. The subtropical planting with palms, grasses and whistling bamboo lends the garden an air of lightness, even on sticky summer days.

This plot is the heart of the Bonnington Square housing development, which was built for railway workers in the 1870s. Derelict in the 1980s, it was occupied by squatters, who subsequently formed a housing cooperative and took over the lease of the buildings. They also formed the Bonnington Square Garden Association – among its members was the garden designer Dan Pearson – after they were informed that the former bombsite on the square was to be sold for development. In 1994 money from the government and the council became available to transform the land into a magical garden. It was named Pleasure Garden in homage to the former Vauxhall Pleasure Gardens, and is even lit by fairy lights at night.

Connected by a secret passage to Bonnington Square is Harleyford Road Community Garden. This garden has a different charm to the Pleasure Garden but is no less appealing. Here, a path paved with mosaics winds through the garden, shaded by overhanging branches leading to a pond, wildlife area, herb and vegetable border and a children's play area. The 1.5-acre site began life in 1984 as a vegetable plot on the site of a former Georgian terrace. Local residents designed the garden in 1986–88 and have maintained it ever since. Nurseries and schools also use it to study nature.

Visit both gardens as they showcase the amazing achievements of the local community spirit.

Address Harleyford Road/Bonnington Square, SW8 1TF ,
www.bonningtonsquaregarden.org.uk | Getting there Tube to Vauxhall (Victoria Line)
or Oval (Northern Line) | Hours Daily dawn–dusk | Tip Walk around Bonnington
Square with its beautiful street gardens and trees and have a coffee at Bonnington Café,
set up by the same co-op that leases the square (11 Vauxhall Grove).

9 _ Broomfield Park

Swiss cheese plant for dessert?

If you stop visiting London's parks and gardens beyond the North Circular you'll be missing out on some lovely ones! Enfield offers the green-seeking visitor a few beautiful spots, and Broomfield Park is a hidden gem. Once part of Broomfield Estate, it belonged in 1566 to a leather merchant named John Bromefylde, whose surname came from the word 'bromfield' meaning an open field where broom grows. In the following centuries the estate changed owners several times, and became the first public park to open in Southgate in 1903. Broomfield House was used by the community for different purposes and was turned into a museum in 1925. Unfortunately a major fire destroyed the house in 1984, and at present there are not enough funds to restore it.

The 52-acre park sits at the heart of the local community. Locals volunteer in the community orchard or enjoy a cup of tea at Palmers Greenery Community Café. The three ornamental lakes were originally fishponds and later part of a baroque water garden. Then, in the early 20th century, one of them was used for swimming and bathing – a tradition many people hope to revive. Broomfield is also home to the oldest model boating pond in Britain. Other features include the Sensory Garden, designed for the visually impaired, and the Garden of Remembrance, commemorating the death of soldiers and civilians in World Wars I and II. In autumn the Long Bed – at 200 m the longest flowerbed in London – blazes with fiery perennials.

The recently replanted conservatory houses bougainvillea and amaryllis as well as more exotic plants such as *Thunbergia mysorensis*, grown at the site from a small seedling, and the Swiss cheese plant *(Monstera deliciosa)*, all of whose parts are poisonous except for the ripe fruit, which supposedly tastes of banana, pineapple and mango.

So, even if you're not a local, it is worth venturing beyond the North Circular!

Address Aldermans Hill, N13 4HE, www.friendsofbroomfieldpark.org, secretary@friendsofbroomfieldpark.org | Getting there Train to Palmers Green (Great Northern) | Hours Mon–Sat 8am–dusk; Sun 8.30am–dusk | Tip What do you think of afternoon tea at Baskervilles Tea Shop (66 Aldermans Hill)?

10_Brown Hart Gardens

Quarrelling forbidden!

There's only 10,000 square feet (929 m²) of it, but Brown Hart Gardens in Mayfair is special for several reasons: you can't see it at street level and have to climb stairs or take a lift to it, as this classically inspired extravaganza sits atop a Grade II listed electricity substation. The question is, how did the garden get up there?

In the late 19th century, following the residential development of Duke Street, a communal garden was created in 1889 between Brown Street and Hart Street. Only 14 years later the second Duke of Westminster leased the space to the Westminster Electric Supply Corporation to build an electricity substation. Although there had been complaints about 'disorderly boys', 'verminous women' and 'tramps', the local residents protested against the loss of this green space. A scheme was suggested to build a garden on top of the transformer chamber. It was designed by C. Stanley Peach in an Italianate style with a stone balustrade and domed neo-baroque pavilions at either end. The mayor of Westminster, Lord Cheylesmore, opened it for the public in June 1906.

The garden was closed in the 1980s and re-opened after refurbishment in 2007. Another renovation in 2013 added a lift, bespoke planters with a seasonal planting scheme and a café, which makes it a favourite lunchtime escape from busy Oxford Street for those in the know. From cinema viewings to Christmas markets, the gardens also host several events during the year.

For anyone who values peace and quiet this place is ideal – not only is it invisible from the street but also unique laws prevent disturbances of the contemplative atmosphere. The plot is part of The Grosvenor Estate whose interesting byelaws state that 'no idle or disorderly person is allowed in the garden' and 'brawling, quarrelling, gambling, playing cards or dice, singing and practicing gymnastics' are prohibited!

Address Duke Street, W1K 6WP, www.grosvenor.com/featured-locations-and-properties/ asset/brown-hart-gardens | **Getting there** Tube to Bond Street (Central and Jubilee Lines) | **Hours** Mon–Sat 8am–8pm; Sun 10am–8pm | **Tip** The Wallace Collection (Manchester Square), famous for its antiques, sculptures and paintings, is a seven-minute walk away (www.wallacecollection.org).

11 Brunswick Square Gardens

Peter Pan's flight path

Brunswick Square Gardens is a small, leafy park surrounded by modern housing blocks in Bloomsbury, London's most literary area. Dominated by mature trees, it appears less flamboyant than some of the other Bloomsbury squares, but just enter and you'll discover that these trees are anything but ordinary! The most majestic of them, the Brunswick Plane, stands in the centre of the garden. It was planted in 1796, is reputed to be the second oldest tree in London and was designated as one of the Great Trees of Britain. There are also two remarkable, much smaller oriental planes, gnarled and pot-bellied, looking like enchanted creatures from a fairy tale.

The square was originally part of Coram's Fields (see ch. 23), and was named after the wife of George II, Caroline of Brunswick, who was supportive of the establishment of the Foundling Hospital there. One of two squares either side of the hospital, its centre was laid out as a garden in 1796–99 and the square quickly became a popular residential area. Even Mr and Mrs Knightley in Jane Austen's novel *Emma* lived here, because the area was 'most favourable as to air'. Unsurprisingly, the literary Bloomsbury Group also left their mark around the square. Virginia Woolf shared a house here with her brother Adrian, the painter Duncan Grant and the economist John Maynard Keynes; and E. M. Forster had his bachelor pad here for many years.

The gardens were neglected after the majority of the surrounding houses were destroyed in the World War II, but re–landscaping took place in 2002–3 and the original railings, also lost in the war, were replaced. Today the Friends of Brunswick Square, formed in 2008, help to maintain and improve the park.

Literature professor Rosemary Ashton has suggested that Peter Pan would have flown over Brunswick Square to reach the Darlings'. Who knows, he might have rested on one of the enchanted planes!

Address Brunswick Square, WC1N 1AN, www.camden.gov.uk/parks | Getting there
Tube to Russell Square (Piccadilly Line) | Hours Daily dawn–dusk | Tip Visit the nearby
Brunswick Centre, an interesting modernist shopping centre with cinema completed in
1972 by Patrick Hodgkinson.

12 Bunhill Fields

Robinsonade for office workers

Bunhill Fields Burial Ground on busy City Road presents a curious sight on sunny days at lunchtime: between rows of closely packed and weathered gravestones, black-suited and -skirted figures sit on benches, stretch out on small green patches of lawn and even lean against the stones, eating.

The name Bunhill Fields, derived from 'bone hill', indicates that this was a Saxon burial site. The ground was also used to bury victims of the plague but was never consecrated, contributing to its popularity with Nonconformists – Christians who practised their faith outside the Church of England – from the 17th century onwards. Some of them were famous writers and artists, among them John Bunyan, author of *Pilgrim's Progress*; Daniel Defoe, author of *Robinson Crusoe;* and the poet, painter and printmaker William Blake.

The grounds were turned into a park in 1865. Today, a railed-off path cuts the cemetery in half in order to channel the lunchtime crowd and protect the headstones. The north part of the 10-acre plot is largely cleared of gravestones, and small patches of lawn alternate with borders of colourful perennials including kniphofia and buddleia at the height of summer. This area – open to visitors – also contains the memorials of Bunyan, Defoe and Blake. Bunyan's grave, topped with an effigy of the man himself, is easily the most elaborate in the cemetery, whereas Blake and his wife share a simple headstone, removed from its original position.

Defoe died in poverty in 1731. A plain headstone also marked the grave he shared with his wife and daughter. During the time the burial ground was closed, lightning struck and destroyed the gravestone. An appeal in the *Christian World* children's newspaper raised enough money to commission a marble obelisk that was finally unveiled in 1870. Today it still seduces office workers to dream their own robinsonades in its shade.

Address 38 City Road, EC1Y 1AU, www.cityoflondon.gov.uk/things-to-do/green-spaces/city-gardens | Getting there Tube to Old Street (Northern Line) | Hours Daily 8am–7pm or to dusk | Tip Visit the adjacent Quaker Garden or John Wesley's House and Chapel just across the road.

13 _ Burgess Park

Park in progress

At 140 acres, Burgess Park is Southwark's largest park. When you visit it today with its lake, wildlife areas, orchard and sports facilities, you can hardly imagine that not so long ago this land was home to factories and built-up residential streets.

The somewhat unusual history of Burgess Park started with the Abercrombie Plan, which was developed by the town planner Sir Patrick Abercrombie in 1943. He found that there weren't enough 'green lungs' for the area and proposed a large park. His plans were put into reality but it took from the 1950s to the 1980s to build the park. Houses were demolished as well as factories such as a lemonade factory and many small, fragmented open spaces were linked together to create the park. Work also went on in the 1990s: thousands of trees were planted, the lake was created, the filled-in canal that ran through the land was greened and sporting facilities were built. They include tennis courts, cricket and football pitches and a BMX track. The park was named after Jessie Burgess, the first female mayor of Camberwell. Another transformation, enabled by a major grant, was completed in 2012.

Some features in the park bear testimony to its domestic and industrial heritage, such as the old lime kiln. Former almshouses in Chumleigh Gardens were turned into a café next to a World Garden with plantings designed to reflect the diversity of the area's population. The Surrey Canal walk follows the old Surrey Canal and is laid out to grow an array of edible plants. Foraging is encouraged! The Glengall Wharf Garden is Burgess Park's food-growing project and welcomes volunteers interested in growing vegetables and other gardening projects. There are also plans to redesign the Grade II listed Passmore Edwards Old Library and Bathhouse and use the building for community spaces. Burgess Park truly is a park in progress.

Address 150 Albany Road, SE5 0AL, www.2.southwark.gov.uk/info/200480/burgess_park | Getting there Tube to Elephant and Castle (Northern and Bakerloo Lines) | Hours Daily dawn–dusk | Tip Fowlds Café offers good food and coffee in an old upholstery shop (3 Addington Square).

14 Bushy Park

Diana or Arethusa?

A hosepipe for a king and a 'Diana' that could be an Arethusa – these are only two of the many interesting features of Bushy Park. Located just north of Hampton Court, the second largest Royal Park covers 1,100 acres of land. The mix of woodland and acid grassland creates a landscape resembling an old-master painting.

Farmland in medieval times, Bushy became Royal in 1529 when it was gifted with Hampton Court to Henry VIII, who immediately turned it into hunting grounds for deer. Large parts of the land have been grazed by deer ever since, creating a unique habitat for many rare and specialised animals and plants. You'll find plants such as harebell, sheep's sorrel and heath bedstraw, and around 123 rare or endangered species of insects. Ground-nesting birds such as skylarks, reed buntings, meadow pipits and stonechats also find the special conditions they need here. The most intriguing animals to watch, though, are the 320 free-roaming red and fallow deer.

Beyond the spectacular wildlife, Bushy Park's Waterhouse Woodland Garden features exotic trees, and the Upper Lodge Water Gardens are in the baroque style. Created in the early 18th century by the first Earl of Halifax they include pools, cascades, basins and a canal, and were partly restored and opened to the public in 2009. The water features in Bushy Park are fed by the Longford River, a canal built by King Charles I in 1638–39 to supply Hampton Court with a steady flow of water. It was nicknamed 'the king's hosepipe'. The canal also feeds the remarkable 'Diana fountain', designed by Hubert Le Sueur for Charles I and placed here by Christopher Wren in 1713 when he created Chestnut Avenue running from the Gates of Hampton Court Palace through the park. Until today it is still disputed if the golden bronze statue topping the fountain depicts Diana, goddess of the hunt or the water nymph Arethusa!

Address Hampton Court Road, Hampton, TW12 2EJ, www.royalparks.org.uk, bushy@royalparks.gsi.gov.uk | Getting there Train to Hampton Court (South West Trains) | Hours Sep & Nov, Mon–Fri 8am–10.30pm; all other months unrestricted | Tip Keep at least 50 metres away from the deer and avoid coming between a mother and her calf or two rutting stags.

15__Calthorpe Project
My garden from home

Entering this garden from noisy Gray's Inn Road via a wooden footbridge you'll step into a separate world. In this 1.5-acre plot you'll find everything a garden needs and more: colourful planted borders, vegetable beds, shaded benches under mature trees, an 'Early Years Garden', a sunken garden, a wild garden with beehives and a pond, a futsal pitch, a plant-growing area and a water fountain. On a summer day you also see people everywhere, gardening, chatting, having lunch or just relaxing.

What makes Calthorpe Project special is not only its diversity and the many different things to do in this relatively small space, but the fact that all this is nearly entirely the result of the effort of local residents.

In 1981, locals received a letter that the Calthorpe site was to be sold for an office development. They leapt into action and started a campaign to find out what people really wanted. Young families wished for somewhere for their children to play, others wanted allotments or just a nice bench to sit on. It soon became obvious that the need for a green space was great, and the garden was built over the next two years with financial support from the council. Today, Calthorpe is not only a beautiful garden. There are also gardening groups for people over 60, Bangladeshi women and people with disabilities; programmes for teenagers and 1-metre-square allotments for people who have no garden.

The biggest problem today is to get sufficient funding to run Calthorpe. As large donations are scarce, a call went out for commercial ideas. The result: a café was founded, the garden can be hired for events, and an anaerobic digester produces energy for the café and helps fertilise crops. Calthorpe also received funding from the Mayor's Pocket Park Project. These commercial activities make it possible for many locals to continue seeing Calthorpe as their back garden!

Address 258-274 Gray's Inn Road, WC1X 8LH, www.calthorpeproject.org.uk, info@calthorpeproject.org.uk | Getting there Tube to King's Cross St. Pancras (Circle, Piccadilly, Metropolitan, Hammersmith & City, Northern and Victoria Lines) | Hours Mon–Fri 10am–6pm; Sat & Sun noon–6pm | Tip Explore the recently opened Postal Museum, nearby on Phoenix Place (www.postalmuseum.org).

16_ Camley Street Natural Park

The King's Cross wilderness

You'll find all kinds of wildlife in this 2-acre nature reserve beside Regent's Canal. Astonishing, as in Victorian times the park was the site of a coal drop, where coal arrived by train to be loaded into canal boats. Even more so because it's only a stone's throw from King's Cross, one of the busiest railway stations in London!

Camley Street was opened as the first urban nature reserve in Europe in 1985, and is managed by the London Wildlife Trust, a charity that aims to protect London's wild spaces. They see urban nature reserves as multifunctional spaces that filter the air, are havens for wildlife, reduce erosion and help people connect with nature. The trust offers activities and events, organises outdoor teaching for schoolchildren, and recruits volunteers – the soul of any park – who do everything from tree coppicing to annual meadow cutting. If you don't come across one of them working, you'll find their stories on panels along your way.

Sign in at the visitor's centre and follow the paths to different habitats. Try your hand at pond dipping (nets and trays are available at the visitor's centre) and discover newts, pond skaters, water boatmen, freshwater shrimps and frogs. In meadows you might spot snake's head fritillaries, orchids or geraniums, depending on the time of year. On the canal, a Floating Forest Garden is anchored, created on an old dredger that collected silt and rubbish from the canal bed. Its 32 square metres house over 100 plant species, including elm trees, different apple varieties, and an edible understory of strawberries! Visitors can observe life on Regent's Canal from the viewing platform and might even spot a kingfisher. There are plans for a footbridge across the canal that will make this urban wilderness even more accessible.

Address 12 Camley Street, N1C 4PW, www.wildlondon.org.uk/reserves | **Getting there**
Tube to King's Cross St. Pancras (Circle, Metropolitan, Piccadilly, Hammersmith & City,
Northern and Victoria Lines) | **Hours** Daily 10am–4pm in winter; 10am–5pm in summer |
Tip For a view over the King's Cross area with all its new developments, go to the viewing
platform on Goods Way opposite Granary Square.

17 __ Canonbury Square

The stolen girl

The *Evening Standard* of 24 May, 1956 described Canonbury Square as 'London's most beautiful square'. The oldest garden square in Islington was created from 1805 to 1830 by Henry Leroux and Richard Laycock on land owned by the Marquess of Northampton. Before it was finished, Canonbury Road was built, cutting the square in two halves. The garden was laid out in 1840. The 4th Marquess of Northampton opened the garden to the public in 1884, and donated it to Islington Council in 1888.

Many famous figures in art and literature lived here, among them Evelyn Waugh who moved to 17a in 1928. The square was not as fashionable then as it had been in the 19th century, but to writer Harold Acton, it was still 'agreeably symmetrical and soothing to the eye'. In the 1950s Duncan Grant and Vanessa Bell lived at 26a. The most famous inhabitant of the square was Eric Arthur Blair, better known by his pen name, George Orwell, who moved to 27b Canonbury Square with his family after their flat in Kilburn was bombed in 1944, and wrote parts of *1984* here. By then Canonbury Square was a bleak tenement in a down-at-heel area, and is said to have inspired the 'decaying home' in the novel.

This all changed again when the gardens were redesigned and enclosed with new reproduction railings (removed during the war) in the 1950s. In 2006 the gardens saw another makeover when the Loire Valley Wines Legacy Gardens planted a small vineyard, roses and lavender in the eastern part of the square. The western part now also impresses with its circular layout, tall palm trees and central urn. The beds are filled with a mixture of lavender, grasses and perennials.

Canonbury Square is again one of the most fashionable parts of Islington. Only one thing is missing: the stolen girl! This Italian statue of a young girl, donated by a Mr Stokes in 1943, was stolen and never recovered.

Address Canonbury Square, N1 2AL, www.islington.gov.uk | Getting there Tube to
Highbury & Islington (Victoria Line) | Hours Daily 8am–dusk | Tip One of the Georgian
buildings in Canonbury Square houses The Estorick Collection of Modern Italian Art
(www.estorickcollection.com).

18__ Chelsea Physic Garden
The power of plants

It's amazing how many different species of plants fit in this four-acre plot near the Thames in Chelsea! Apart from its size, Chelsea Physic Garden is a garden of superlatives. Founded in 1673, it is the oldest botanical garden in London and the second oldest in Britain. In its walls it contains around 5,000 different medicinal, edible or otherwise useful plants, as well as the oldest English alpine garden and the largest outdoor fruiting olive tree.

The glasshouses contain tropical and subtropical plants and the mild microclimate allows the growth of an outdoor grapefruit tree, pomegranates, mulberries and other plants that are not usually found in Britain. Medicinal plants abound as well, some of which provide compounds used in medicine today such as woolly foxglove (*Digitalis lanata*), used to strengthen and control the heartbeat, and broad bean *(Vicia faba)*, which helps to control the symptoms of Parkinson's disease. The Garden of Edible and Useful Plants – beautifully laid out with brick paths inspired by 18th-century gardens – contains an even wider range of plants, and a small vineyard. Here you can learn the origins of modern vegetables and which aromatic plants are used in perfume, and marvel at the many applications of single plants, such as cotton. With cells 2,000 times longer than wide, its applications range from textiles and cosmetics to chewing gum and explosives, the latest being the use of its seed's component gossypol as a male oral contraceptive.

For Head Gardener Nick Bailey the garden is constantly evolving. His aim is to make it more accessible to a contemporary audience. One of his new developments is the World Woodland Garden, opened in 2015 with 15 different species of snowdrop on display from the end of January onwards. It shows that Chelsea can be both a peaceful haven for enjoyment and a demonstration of the importance and power of plants.

Address 66 Royal Hospital Road, SW3 4HS, www.chelseaphysicgarden.co.uk, enquiries@chelseaphysicgarden.co.uk | Getting there Tube to Sloane Square (District and Circle Lines) | Hours Please check the website. | Tip Don't miss the Chelsea Flower Show, which takes place every year in May in the grounds of the Royal Hospital, Chelsea (Royal Hospital Road).

19___Chiswick House

From goose foot to Beatles

18th century gardens seldom come any better than this. Created in 1729 in the Neo-Palladian style, they emulate ancient Roman gardens such as Hadrian's Villa Adriana at Tivoli. Chiswick's owner, 'The Architect Earl' Lord Burlington, brought architect and landscape designer William Kent back from his second Grand Tour of Italy and set him to work.

Kent took inspiration from Nicolas Poussin's and Claude Lorrain's landscape paintings, and his designs for many vistas were intended to resemble paintings. Artists from all over Europe visited the gardens to turn them into paintings once again.

The original Jacobean outline was replaced with 65 acres of grass and woodland in the new 'natural' style, complete with columns; temples; grand vistas; a lake, cascade and bridge; a hedge theatre and countless statues and garden buildings influenced by Renaissance, Roman and Greek architecture. It's not surprising that Chiswick became the birthplace of the English landscape movement and inspired Blenheim Palace and Central Park in New York.

One of the most interesting parts of the garden is the *patte d'oie* or goose foot: three radiating avenues lined with hedges that resemble the webbed foot of a goose, each leading to structures of architectural interest, of which only one, the Rustic House, survives.

A 19th century addition to the gardens is the beautiful conservatory created by Samuel Ware in 1813. At the time the longest of its kind, it houses the oldest camellia collection in England, some of which were planted in 1828. The half-circular Italian Garden in front of it was designed by Lewis Kennedy in 1812 for the so-called Bachelor Duke (6th Duke of Devonshire).

The beauty of the gardens impressed not only 18th and 19th century visitors. In 1966 the Beatles came here to film the music video for their songs *Paperback Writer* and *Rain*.

Address Burlington Lane, W4 2RP, www.chgt.org.uk | Getting there Train to Chiswick (South West Trains) | Hours Daily 7am–dusk | Tip Visit Chiswick from 3 March to 2 April to see the camellias in full bloom (conservatory opens daily 10am–4pm).

20 Christchurch Greyfriars
The garden of queens

The ruin and tower of Christchurch Greyfriars provide a dramatic background to this beautiful garden, which is planted in the nave of the former church. A major refurbishment in 2011 resulted in its current appearance. On both sides of a central path leading to the west tower, densely planted borders are edged by a low box hedge. Ten tall wooden towers play host to clematis and climbing roses, and represent the former pillars that supported the roof of the church. The soft colour scheme of mainly blue, purple and white perennials adds a romantic touch to the setting. Tourists and office workers come here to rest, eat their lunches or just enjoy the peaceful atmosphere. Little do they know that the history of this place wasn't always so peaceful!

The Franciscan church of Greyfriars was built on the site in 1225, and was the second-largest medieval church in London. Several English queens were buried here, among them Margaret of France, who supported the building of the church. Her half-niece Isabella of France, also called the 'She-Wolf of France' because she deposed her husband, Edward II, and probably even murdered him, is buried here as well. It is said that her ghost haunts the site, clutching the heart of her murdered husband. Another spectre to haunt the churchyard is that of 'The Mad Maid of Kent', Elizabeth Barton, who was hanged and buried here after she made some not very well-received prophecies about Henry VIII and Anne Boleyn.

In 1666 the medieval church burnt down during the Great Fire and a much smaller replacement was designed by Christopher Wren and completed in 1687. It became a musical centre where Felix Mendelssohn and Samuel Wesley performed. The church was destroyed a second time in 1940 during the Blitz, leaving only the tower and the walls standing. Sitting in this peaceful garden today, it is difficult to imagine its past upheavals.

Address King Edward Street, EC1A 7BA | Getting there Tube to St Paul's (Central Line) | Hours Unrestricted | Tip The Monument (Paternoster Square) commemorates the Great Fire of London. It has a viewing platform at the top.

21__Cleary Gardens
The Loire Valley in London

This terraced green space of roughly a third of an acre is one of a number of inner-city gardens that are small in size but provide vital breathing space for humans and wildlife in the capital. It owes its existence to the Blitz, and to some very dedicated London citizens. Every single building on the site was destroyed in World War II, and the shoemaker Joseph Brandis saw an opportunity to create a new garden here. His hands-on approach included carrying mud from the riverbank and soil from his own garden to be used on the plot.

Since then the garden has developed greatly. It was re-landscaped from 1985 to 1988 with brick pergolas, lawns, trees, shrubs and palms, and renamed after Frederick Cleary (1905–1984), the chairman of the Metropolitan Public Gardens Association, which funded the refurbishment for its centenary. Cleary planted a golden acacia in the garden in 1982. A firm local favourite is the bed of 200 Yatsuka tree peonies next to the top pergola, flowering spectacularly in late spring. They were given to the City of London in 2006 by the Japanese island of Daikonjima.

The terraced layout of the garden represents different eras of London's history, and the different uses of the site over time. A retaining wall of a Roman bath was found in 1964, and evidence also indicates that medieval vintners grew and traded vines here. In line with this tradition, the planting of vines in the gardens was renewed in 2007 under the Loire Valley Wines Legacy Garden scheme, a refurbishment that also included aromatic shrubs, climbers and flowering plants reminiscent of the Loire Valley landscape.

Not only humans find this little oasis attractive. Dunnocks, house sparrows, blackbirds and blue tits are often seen, with some pairs nesting in the buddleias growing on the walls.

Sitting here on a bench under the pergola makes the Loire Valley seem to be just around the corner!

Address Queen Victoria Street/Huggin Hill, EC4V 4HQ, www.cityoflondon.gov.uk | Getting there Tube to Mansion House (District and Circle Lines) | Hours Daily 8am–7pm or to dusk, whichever is earlier | Tip Check out nearby Whittington Garden, a small garden next to St Michael Paternoster Royal, rebuilt by Christopher Wren in 1694 (College Street/ Upper Thames Street).

22___Clissold Park
Lovers reunited

Like many of London's green spaces, Clissold Park began its life as part of an estate. Slighty elevated, the graceful 18th century manor next to the spire of St Mary's Church could easily preside over a small village – but here we are in Stoke Newington in London's borough of Hackney!

Originally called Paradise House, Clissold House was built in 1790 by the banker Jonathan Hoare, who originated from an Irish Quaker family. Two pits on the land provided bricks for the house and are now Beckmere Lake and Runtzmere Lake, after Joseph Beck and John Runtz who campaigned to turn the estate into a public park in the late 19th century. But the love story that resulted in the Clissold name happened earlier. When Jonathan Hoare ran into financial difficulties, the estate was sold to William Crawshay, an upstart industrialist, in 1811. Crawshay refused to give permission for his daughter Eliza to marry the love of her life, Augustus Clissold, a lowly curate. Her father soon died, Eliza married Clissold, and the house and park were renamed in his honour.

Today the house serves as a café and community space for locals and visitors. In front of it, a small part of the New River (see New River Walk, ch. 69) is brimming with different varieties of waterfowl, such as tufted, redhead and white ducks, and Egyptian and Canada geese. Further attractions are the animal enclosures containing fallow deer and goats, a small butterfly dome (open only in the summer), a paddling pool, tennis courts and a skate park.

After a rough time in the 1980s and 90s an injection of Heritage Lottery money gave the house and park new life. Now new generations of children can splash in the paddling pool, climb trees, have their first dates and push their own children around in prams. Eliza and Augustus Clissold never had children, but they probably wouldn't have minded this use of their estate!

Address Green Lanes, N16 9HJ, www.hackney.gov.uk/clissold-park, parks@hackney.gov.uk | Getting there Tube to Finsbury Park (Victoria Line) then bus 106 towards Whitechapel to Green Lanes | Hours Daily from 7.30am, closing times vary, please check website. | Tip The nearby Old Church is the only surviving Elizabethan church in London.

23 _ Coram's Fields

No unaccompanied adults!

A wrought-iron fence and large gates enclose this seven-acre green space. A glimpse through the iron bars reveals an attractive pavilion, plane trees, lawns and benches. It looks tempting, but you can't just enter this park. A sign clearly states that you have to be less than 16 years old or accompanied by a child to visit.

Coram's Fields is a truly unique garden and playground. Its history dates back to the Foundling Hospital that existed here in the 18th century. Captain Thomas Coram founded the home for destitute and abandoned children in 1739. Among its benefactors were Friedrich Handel and William Hogarth, and even Charles Dickens attended services in the hospital chapel. Later the hospital moved out of London and the buildings were demolished, but following public protests the site was saved and redeveloped as London's first public children's playground, opening in 1936. The Harmsworth Memorial Pavilion was built at the same time as an elaborate playground shelter with a relief of playing children and a rooftop clock.

Today Coram's Fields offers play areas for different ages, a large adventure playground with an aerial slide, a sandpit and a paddling pool in the summer. There is a drop-in centre for under fives and a community nursery, as well as a youth centre for older children with an arts studio, a music studio and an open space for dance and other activities. At the little city farm, children can see goats, chickens, rabbits and birds.

Coram's Fields is run by an independent charitable trust that also organises an after-school play scheme and different sport activities. Their exciting master plan for the site includes water-play fountains, a rockery adventure area, new sports courts and the relocation of the café to the Harmsworth Memorial Pavilion. Tell the kids that, for once, you won't be taking them; they'll be taking you!

Address 93 Guilford Street, WC1N 1DN, www.coramsfields.org | Getting there Tube to Russell Square (Piccadilly Line) | Hours Daily 9am–dusk | Tip Visit the Foundling Museum and learn the story of the Foundling Hospital (40 Brunswick Square).

24 Crystal Palace Park

Pleasure, discovery and invention

This park exudes the Victorian spirit of invention and innovation. While the magnificent glass and iron structure of the palace is long gone, many of the features here – from the crumbling stone terraces adorned with sphinxes, to the maze, lakes and dinosaur collection – show traces of Victorian splendour.

Designed to house the Crystal Palace, which had been created for the Great Exhibition in Hyde Park in 1851, the park's pleasure grounds were developed between 1852 and 1855 by Sir Joseph Paxton. Edward Milner created the Great Maze, English Landscape Garden and Italian Garden, with lakes and waterworks. Another new attraction must have scared Victorian visitors senseless: the Crystal Palace Dinosaurs, life-size prehistoric models lurking behind bushes, feeding at the lake and rubbing themselves against trees. Created by Benjamin Waterhouse Hawkins, they were the first life-size dinosaur models the public had ever seen.

Queen Victoria opened the palace and park in a grand ceremony complete with firework displays and performances in June 1854. In 1895 a football stadium opened, and was used for the 1914 FA Cup final. The 1911 Festival of the Empire saw a railway installed and several buildings erected to represent the Empire. Unfortunately, Crystal Palace burned down completely in 1936 and in the following years the park became derelict. In the 1960s it found new life as a 'sports park' with its Athletics Stadium and National Sports Centre. Its Victorian features still needed rejuvenation, however. Works to restore the dinosaurs started in 2001; in 2006 Capel Manor College opened a centre in the park including a model farm with animals. There are further plans to restore the crumbling terraces and to create new gardens.

Crystal Palace Park clearly has the capacity to adapt to whatever pleasures, discoveries or inventions epitomise the spirit of the time.

Address Thicket Road, SE19 2GA, www.bromley.gov.uk | **Getting there** London Overground to Crystal Palace (East London Line) | **Hours** Mon–Fri 7.30am–dusk; Sat & Sun 9am–dusk | **Tip** The Crystal Palace Museum showcases the history of the famous glass building (open Sun 11am–3pm).

25 Culpeper Community Garden

By and for local people

A few minutes' walk from Angel Station on Cloudesley Road, a small iron gate is set between tall walls. Above it a sign welcomes the visitor to 'Culpeper Community Garden cultivated by and for local people'. A few steps lead down into a different world. Behind a lawn, dragonflies hover over rushes in a small pond; off to the right a small dry garden bathes in the sun. Narrow paths lead into the garden's depths, hidden by tall trees and bushes, revealing further surprises: a rose walk, a rockery, a wildlife garden and 56 small plots looked after by locals. Each has its own individual style depending on its gardener. Some are very ornamental with clipped topiary, others offer a riot of colour or are planted with exotic edible crops. There are benches everywhere, and as the garden is open to the public you may also encounter office workers having lunch on the lawn. Maintained by volunteers and two paid garden workers, the less-than-half-acre plot is densely planted; foxgloves, roses and forget-me-nots lend it a cottage-garden feel in early summer.

Set up in 1982, Culpeper is one of the oldest community gardens in London. It was the brainchild of the schoolteacher Anthea Douglas, who discovered the derelict bombsite on her way to work. Her idea was to create a garden for her schoolchildren and the local community. Lots of local initiative and the support of the council made the garden possible. The now mature trees were planted by schoolchildren and the plots were allocated to locals who had no garden. The site is now managed by an annually elected committee following organic gardening principles.

The multi-award-winning Culpepper coordinates with various community groups, organising many events throughout the year: craft workshops, storytelling workshops, the annual pensioners' strawberry tea and a summer arts week, just to name a few. A true community garden!

Address 1 Cloudesley Road, N1 0EG, www.culpeper.org.uk, gardenworker@gmail.com | Getting there Tube to Angel (Northern Line) | Hours Daily 8am–7pm | Tip On Wednesdays and Saturdays there is an antique market in nearby Camden Passage.

26_Dalston Eastern Curve Garden

New life at the Eastern Curve

Urban Dalston, near Dalston Junction, is not an area where you would expect a garden, but turn into Dalston Lane and you'll soon spot a huge mural of the 1983 peace carnival – painted in 1985 by Mick Jones and Ray Walker. Open the bright green door next to it and you'll enter a completely different world. The noise and the exhaust fumes of the busy road fall away and breathing becomes easier. The open green space is filled with flowers, fruit trees, quirky nesting boxes, plants in every conceivable container and children's artworks hanging from trees or stuck in raised borders. Stanley, the resident cat, will probably greet you, and suddenly you'll have all the time in the world to wander around. You'll come across the Pineapple House, a beautiful greenhouse with a wood-burning stove that offers shelter in the winter. The wildlife-friendly planting here consists of native hedgerows, wild cherry, silver birch, alder and hazel. Raised beds are filled with vegetables and tempting raspberries and strawberries. At the back, an open space surrounded by butterfly bushes buzzes with insects in summer. The garden offers contact with nature in an area with few open spaces.

The café, situated in a wooden pavilion, offers soup made from locally grown organic vegetables, soda bread and cakes. In the winter there's mulled wine and spiced cider, and no worries – they also provide blankets and hot-water bottles to keep you warm! The café is run by Grow Cook Eat, a Dalston initiative that helped to set up the garden in 2010. The many activities in the garden – from gardening volunteering sessions to yoga and flower arranging to Halloween pumpkin carving – are run by volunteers, members of the Hackney community breathing new life into the former site of the Eastern Curve Railway, derelict for half a century.

Address 13 Dalston Lane, E8 3DF, www.dalstongarden.org, info@dalstongarden.org | **Getting there** London Overground to Dalston Junction (East London Line) or Dalston Kingsland (North London Line) | **Hours** Mon–Thu 11am–7pm; Fri & Sat 11am–10pm; Sun 11am–9pm; please check website | **Tip** On warm summer nights visit Dalston Roof Park (18-22 Ashwin Street, closed in winter).

27 Dulwich Picture Gallery
Walking the dog

Britain's first purpose-built public art gallery opened to the public in 1817. It was founded by Sir Francis Bourgeois, court painter to George III, and built by his friend Sir John Soane (1753–1837).

Bourgeois was not only a painter but also an art dealer and collector. Together with Margaret and Noel Desenfans he formed an art collection for King Stanislaus Augustus of Poland, but by the time they had finished, Poland had disappeared as a country and the king was forced to abdicate.

Bourgeois and the Desenfans looked for a home for their Royal Collection, and after the death of Noel Desenfans, Bourgeois became the sole owner of the collection and bequeathed it to Dulwich College with the stipulation that it be open to the public. The gallery, a mausoleum for Bourgeois and Desenfans and almshouses were built.

Between 1909 and 1939 almshouses in the college grounds were converted into new gallery space. Further repairs were made after damage in World War II, and in 1999–2000 Rick Mather Architects renovated the buildings and built a new extension for visitors.

This also led to a re-landscaping of the three-acre garden with lawns, winding paths, trees and shrubs. In autumn, beautiful acers turn the garden fiery red. The collection of trees includes black mulberry *(Morus nigra)*, dawn redwood (*Metasequoia glyptostroboides)* and Kentucky coffeetree (*Gymnocladus dioicus)*. The garden has become an extension of the museum, an open-air gallery, and the space has seen some brilliant art installations over the years. In 2012 the artist Philip Haas installed four 15-foot fibreglass sculptures inspired by Arcimboldo's paintings of the four seasons. In 2016 the exhibition of the Norwegian painter Nikolai Astrup was celebrated by a week of fire sculptures. Visitors sometimes mull over the name of the first contemporary sculpture the gallery acquired. The three carved boulders by Peter Randall-Page are called *Walking the Dog*.

Address Gallery Road, SE21 7AD, www.dulwichpicturegallery.org.uk,
enquiries@dulwichpicturegallery.org.uk | Getting there Train to West Dulwich
(Thameslink, Southeastern) | Hours Tue–Sun 10am–5pm | Tip After a visit
to the gallery and garden hire a pedalo at nearby Dulwich Park.

28 Duncan Terrace Gardens

Fashionable living for birds

These long, narrow gardens, sandwiched between attractive Georgian terraces, are not only full of vibrant plants, such as the red firethorn berries that glow in the autumn sun, but also have a colourful history. In the 18th and early 19th century, before the site was fully developed, it featured a nursery for exotic plants, and the essayist Charles Lamb and his sister lived in a cottage so close to the river that one of their guests accidently fell in when he left the house without glasses. Later inhabitants included painter Walter Sickert and science-fiction writer Douglas Adams. Today the rows of Georgian houses form one of London's most fashionable living areas; one of their best-known inhabitants is politician Boris Johnson.

Duncan Terrace and Colebrooke Row belong to a number of green spaces in Islington following the New River (see New River Walk, ch. 69), which once ran between them. When Duncan Terrace became a public garden in 1892, the riverbed was already filled in. Landscape designer Fanny Wilkinson planted weeping willow over a winding path, reminding visitors of the river that flowed underneath. Most likely she also installed the limestone rocks edging the Colebrooke Gardens path.

The gardens were rejuvenated in 2007 – 8 with over 1,000 flowering shrubs, trees, ferns and herbaceous perennials. In spring the borders are filled with hellebores, dicentra and lily of the valley; in summer the perennials come into their own and Japanese anemones can be seen flowering until late autumn.

Drawing more than human visitors is an installation by London Fieldworks called *Spontaneous City*, wherein 300 wooden bird boxes are installed in a tree of heaven, providing shelter for birds, bees and insects. The box installation was inspired by the surrounding Georgian houses and 1960s flats. No wonder this is a desirable living area even among robins and blue tits!

Address Duncan Terrace and Colebrooke Row, N1 8AL, duncanterraceandcolebrookerowgardens.com | **Getting there** Tube to Angel (Northern Line) | **Hours** Daily 8am–dusk | **Tip** There is a small, rose-filled garden on Elia Mews, just around the corner from Colebrooke Row.

29 Eltham Palace and Gardens

A strange beauty

Royal residence – farm – ruin – art deco manor house – museum: Eltham Palace and Gardens' colourful history is visible at different levels of the 19-acre garden, and is a major part of its attraction. The moated manor house including dovecote, deer park and windmill came into royal possession in 1305 when the Bishop of Durham granted it to Edward, Prince of Wales. The following two Edwards improved and extended the building and park. Richard II built the stone bridge that is today the oldest stone bridge in London still in use. The surrounding parkland was a popular hunting ground with several kings until Henry VIII abandoned this palace in favour of Greenwich Palace.

In the following centuries the buildings were demolished and the parks stripped of trees and used as farmland. The palace became a romantic ruin, painted by artists. The beautiful Great Hall was restored in 1828 and again in 1911 – 14, but grandeur returned only in 1933 when Stephen and Virginia Courtauld leased the site from the crown and began repairs and building work. Architects Seely and Paget created a stylish garden to match the lavish new art deco house, adding new areas to the existing design and structure. One of these areas was a part of the moat, which was refilled with water. A very fashionable rock garden with a cascade was created on its bank. Further additions were a sunken rose garden and a woodland garden. The stone columns of the wisteria-covered pergola were salvaged from the Bank of England in the 1930s.

A 21st century addition is the long, 1930s-style herbaceous border at the foot of the south moat wall, designed by Isabelle van Groeningen. The contrast here between medieval and art deco, with traces of other eras thrown in, is strangely charming. The different styles don't mix, but complement and enhance each other's beauty.

Address Court Yard, Eltham, Greenwich, SE9 5QE, www.english-heritage.org.uk/visit/places/eltham-palace-and-gardens | Getting there Train to Mottingham (Southeastern) | Hours Please check website for opening times. | Tip Did you know that Eltham Palace is one of the most haunted castles in Britain? The ghost of a former servant is giving guided tours at night!

30__Fenton House and Garden
Up to greener pastures!

The elevated village of Hampstead with its better air than Central London, its medicinal wells and large green expanse of Hampstead Heath became popular among the wealthy middle class in the 17th and 18th century. They started moving to more rural areas, and Fenton House and its garden bear testimony to that fashion. Built at the end of the 17th century, the 'substantial brick building' has 'a pleasant garden well planted with fruit-trees, and a kitchen-garden all inclos'd with a substantial brick wall'.

The house changed hands several times, most of its proprietors being wealthy merchants. Lady Binning, the last private owner, bequeathed the property to the National Trust. Today it is a museum housing her porcelain collection as well as the Benton Fletcher collection of keyboard instruments.

The layout of the walled garden hasn't changed much since the 1860s. An acacia-lined path runs from the wrought-iron gates up to the house and the visitor enters the garden to the north of the house through a rectangular opening in a tall yew hedge. Only now the structure of this enchanting garden – divided by box hedges and perimeter paths – is revealed, containing a flower garden, a sunken garden, a rose garden, a working kitchen garden and a 300-year-old orchard. A raised terrace walk runs along the old brick wall covered with climbing roses, ceanothus, wisteria and an old espalier pear tree. In May it's a sea of purple alliums and in the summer perennials in silver, blue, pink and pale yellow dominate the border. The rose garden continues the soft English colour scheme but the most charming part of the garden is the orchard in spring where old apple varieties such as Beauty of Bath or Pitmaston Pine Apple are underplanted with tulips and forget-me-nots. Come and forget being only a short distance away from the inner city; imagine yourself in greener pastures.

Address Hampstead Grove, NW3 6SP, www.nationaltrust.org.uk | **Getting there** Tube to Hampstead (Northern Line) | **Hours** Wed–Sun 11am–5pm; closed Nov & Dec | **Tip** The museum is worth a visit and you will get the view of the garden (and other parts of Hampstead) from a small balcony at the top of the house.

31 __ Finsbury Park
Fit in Finsbury

Once part of the ancient Forest of Middlesex where the Bishops of London hunted, Finsbury Park was opened to the public in 1869. Most of its ornamental features were designed by the landscape designer Alexander McKenzie, including the American Gardens with their old rhododendrons and azaleas and the McKenzie Flower Garden with its formal square with circular and diamond-shaped flower beds to both sides. The 115-acre park with a boating lake, bandstand, chrysanthemum house and sporting facilities became very popular.

The park has since seen its fair share of ups and downs. World War I saw large peace demonstrations with Sylvia Pankhurst as one of the speakers taking place here. The bandstand was destroyed by an elephant, and then during World War II anti-aircraft predictor guns were placed on the running track. In the 1990s the park happily became a popular venue for rock concerts by the likes of The Sex Pistols, Oasis and Bob Dylan, but at the same time public services were cut and sadly it became run-down and unsafe.

A major grant from the Heritage Lottery in 2005 enabled desperately needed restorations including the re-landscaping of the American Garden and a reconstruction of the original McKenzie Flower Garden. The funds also helped re-establish the sporting facilities that initially made Finsbury Park so popular. Before it became a public park, bowls, archery and pigeon shooting were already being practised here. Now a new outdoor gym with 14 pieces of equipment and 20 exercise stations can be enjoyed in the northeast area of the park. There are also seven tennis courts, a running track, a walking trail, a skate park, a bowling green and sports pitches. It's no wonder the park is home to football, basketball, baseball and softball clubs, and professional runners and cyclists practise here. If that's not an incentive to get fit in Finsbury Park, what is?

Address Endymion Road, N4, www.haringey.gov.uk/finsbury-park, parks@haringey.gov.uk | Getting there Tube to Manor House (Piccadilly Line) | Hours Daily dawn – dusk | Tip The Castle Climbing Centre on Green Lanes offers 450 climbing routes and 90 roped lines (www.castle-climbing.co.uk).

32 Fulham Palace

Ecclesial splendour or sandy beach?

Since Bishop Waldhere acquired the land in 700, until Bishop Stopford retired in 1975, generations of bishops wandered the grounds of Fulham Palace Gardens and Bishop's Park along the south bank of the River Thames in Lambeth. Fulham Palace was used as a summer residence for the Bishop of London, and was once surrounded by a two-kilometre moat with possibly pre-Roman origins. The current buildings on the site are a mixture of styles and periods: Tudor manor house, Georgian additions and a Victorian chapel.

Over the centuries many of the bishops contributed to the gardens. Among the most notable were Bishop Grindal (1559–1570) who brought the first tamarisk tree to the garden. He also annually provided grapes for Elizabeth I's table. Bishop Compton (1675–1730) was a keen botanist who sent out plant collectors to the colonies and planted many exotic specimens. The first magnolia *(Magnolia virginiana)* in Europe was grown here as well as the first cork oak *(Quercus suber),* black walnut *(Juglans nigra),* Judas tree and tulip tree. Later bishops improved or reshaped the gardens. Some were more interested in edible plants to which the large walled garden that still delivers fruit and vegetables in abundance bears testimony. It also features a knot garden that was replanted in 2012 and an impressive wisteria. *The Bishop's Tree* was sculpted by Andrew Frost from a stump of a cedar of Lebanon depicting several bishops and their animals. Other highlights include the late-summer-flowering Bishop dahlias and the recently restored vinery.

Families sated with ecclesial splendour can visit the adjacent Bishop's Park, once also part of the estate. It became a public park in 1893 following a rise in the local population and was extended in 1900 and 1903. It features an ornamental lake, bandstand, rose garden and sport facilities, but it is the water-play feature and 'sandy beach' that make it a favourite with families.

Address Bishop's Avenue, Fulham, SW6 6EA, www.fulhampalace.org | Getting there Tube to Putney Bridge (District Line) | Hours Daily dawn–dusk | Tip Visit the museum in the palace, or walk along the Thames to Pryor's Park.

33 Garden Museum Garden

Anything that is strange

The beautifully carved tomb of the Tradescant family is the centre-piece of this garden in the old churchyard of St Mary-at-Lambeth. The Tradescant family played an important role in garden history. John Tradescant the elder (1570–1638) was head gardener to Robert Cecil at Hatfield House. Later he became gardener to the Duke of Buckingham and to Charles I. He travelled to Russia, North Africa and other countries and brought back many plants and other 'curiosities'. He also encouraged other travellers to bring back their finds and opened Tradescant's Ark, the first public museum in England. His son continued his legacy and travelled to North America to collect trees and plants. Many well-known garden plants were introduced by the Tradescants, among them horse chestnuts, daffodils, hellebores and runner beans. The tomb features high relief carvings of trees at its corners and depicts Egyptian scenes as well as objects from the Tradescant collection along the sides.

The Garden Museum in the church was set up in 1977 to rescue the ancient building from demolition. In 1981 Lady Salisbury, whose husband was a descendant of Robert Cecil, designed a 17th century knot garden around the Tradescant tomb, using species that were either introduced by the Tradescants or cultivated in their garden in Lambeth. The tomb was recarved and its original lid is displayed in the Garden Museum.

The museum and garden was brought into the 21st century in 2016–17 with a re-design of the museum with more gallery space and a re-creation of John Tradescant's Ark. The opening of the medieval church tower with beautiful views over London is also part of the development project. The garden, now containing pavilions dedicated to learning and community work and a play area, was redesigned by Dan Pearson. Tradescant aimed to collect 'anything that is strange'. What gardener wouldn't agree with that?

Address 5 Lambeth Palace Road, SE1 7LB, www.gardenmuseum.org.uk, info@gardenmuseum.org.uk | Getting there Tube to Lambeth North (Bakerloo Line) | Hours Please check website for opening times. | Tip Cross the Thames on Lambeth Bridge, which is painted red to match the red benches in the House of Lords (Westminster Bridge is painted green to match the benches in the House of Commons).

34 __ Geffrye Museum Gardens

A time machine

This 'museum of the home' exhibits London living rooms from 1600 to today. It is set in the last remaining almshouses in Old Shoreditch, built between 1712 and 1714 by the Ironmongers' Company with a bequest from Sir Robert Geffrye, a former mayor of London. Leading Arts and Crafts movement members persuaded the council to convert the buildings into a museum in 1914.

Whereas the front garden of the museum retains its 18th century layout, the back gardens were transformed in 1992–98 into a series of garden rooms. The Herb Garden opened in 1992 with a central fountain by ceramicist Kate Malone in the centre. Brick paths divide it into a traditional pattern of squares and rectangles. Here you can rediscover herbs and flowers, such as clove pinks, that the Tudors put in their salads, and learn that cowslip made a 17th century facial wash.

The success of the award-winning Herb Garden was followed by the creation of a series of period gardens in 1998. They are modelled on middle-class domestic gardens and complement the museum's period rooms. While the 17th century garden is dominated by useful plants like small fruit trees, herbs and vegetables, known as pot herbs, the 18th century garden is a space for promenading and entertaining, with clipped box hedges and gravel paths. A great feature is the 'auricula theatre', a kind of shelf where tender plants can be protected and displayed. The 19th century saw the introduction of more exotic plants and this garden also features a greenhouse where bananas, citrus plants, ferns and bougainvilleas grow. The next garden room displays the more relaxed gardening style of the 20th century influenced by the Arts and Crafts movement and the garden designer Gertrude Jekyll with a wisteria-covered pergola and plenty of roses.

The Geffreye Museum transports visitors back into the past – and the gardens bring it to life.

Address 136 Kingsland Road, E2 8EA, +44 (0)20 7739 9893, www.geffrye-museum.org.uk, info@geffrye-museum.org.uk | Getting there London Overground to Hoxton (East London Line) | Hours The Period Gardens are closed during winter. Please check website for opening times. | Tip Kingsland Road is a hub for Vietnamese restaurants. It's also known as the 'Pho Mile'.

35_ Geraldine Mary Harmsworth Park

For the mothers of Southwark

In 1597 the herbalist John Gerard found water violets on this once marshy site of streams and ponds previously known as St George's Fields. Only lowly houses existed here until serious development began at the end of the 18th century. The land was drained, and in 1815 the Bethlem Royal Hospital, the first psychiatric institution in Europe, was built.

Lord Rothermere, the proprietor of the *Daily Mail* newspaper group, bought the land in 1926 when the hospital relocated, and donated it to the London County Council to create a public park in memory of his adored mother, Geraldine Mary Harmsworth, in 1934. In 1936, the Imperial War Museum opened in the remains of the hospital buildings.

Today this 14.5-acre park is one of the most interesting green spaces in South London. It includes the Imperial War Museum and Tibetan Peace Garden (see ch. 100), as well as a community orchard. The orchard was planted in 2003 with olive, fig, medlar, crab apple quince and strawberry trees so that the diverse community of local children could enjoy fruits from their native countries.

The World Garden comprises plants from subtropical, Mediter-ranean, Alpine and desert climates with cacti, yuccas, bamboo and banana plants. It also includes habitats for stag beetles and the rare London hairy buttercup. The Ice Age Tree Trail informs about pio-neer trees in Britain such as Scotch pine, juniper and birch.

Geraldine Mary Harmsworth would have appreciated such a park in her neighbourhood, especially as she brought up 14 children on her own after her husband died. Until today the park is therefore dedicated to 'the splendid struggling mothers of Southwark in the training and upbringing of their children'.

Address Kennington Road, SE1, www.southwark.gov.uk/parks-and-open-spaces/parks | Getting there Tube to Elephant & Castle (Bakerloo and Northern Lines) | Hours Daily from 7.30am, closing times vary, please check website. | Tip Are you interested in feminism? Try the Feminist Library, which holds an extensive collection of feminist literature (5 Westminster Bridge Road).

36__Gillespie Park

From black to green

Once a railway siding used for sorting coal and later the site of an ink factory opened by Henry C. Stephens (see ch. 97), Gillespie Park sports a pretty black history. It makes it even more astonishing that it is now one of the greenest spots in Islington, a haven in a borough with very few green spaces.

The creation of this seven-acre nature reserve and wildlife park began in the 1980s as a result of a community protest against turning the site into blocks of flats. It finally became a designated nature reserve in 1996, supporting a variety of woodland, pond and meadow habitats. In the 1990s an Ecology Centre was added, built with sustainable softwood, featuring solar panels and painted with organic paints. In co-operation with nurseries and schools, children are introduced to the plants and wildlife here. The centre also runs wildlife gardening workshops and organises a number of annual events, which attract the local community. It is managed by a group of 20 volunteers who invest many hours of free labour, coppicing, cutting hedges or clearing up the ponds.

Many visitors come here for a break from noisy roads and pollution. Entering the woodland through an arch you will suddenly hear not much else than birds singing, among them blue tits, great tits and wrens. In spring you'll find daffodils and primroses; see orchids and lupines on the meadows in early summer and evening primroses in August and September. The ponds are covered with water lilies, and anyone who sits here for a while can observe dragonflies, water soldiers, toads, newts or frogs.

The range of plants and animals here is amazing, counting 244 plant species, over 20 different butterfly and 90 different bird species! It was a proud moment for all the volunteers and friends of Gillespie Park when they could recently celebrate the 20th anniversary of this beautiful urban nature reserve.

Address 191 Drayton Park, N5 1PH, myparks.westminster.gov.uk,
ecologycentre@islington.gov.uk | Getting there Tube to Arsenal (Piccadilly Line) | Hours
Park: daily 8am–dusk; Ecology Centre: Mon–Fri 10am–4pm | Tip Arsenal Football
Stadium is of course just across the road and the park is closed on Arsenal match days!

37__Golden Square
Region of song and smoke

This is the name Charles Dickens gave the area around Golden Square in his novel *The Life and Adventures of Nicholas Nickleby*. He also describes the square: 'Its boarding-houses are musical, and the notes of pianos and harps float in the evening time round the head of the mournful statue, the guardian genius of a little wilderness of shrubs, in the centre of the square.' The square also features in Thomas de Quincey's Confessions of an English Opium Eater.

Originally named Gelding Close, as the land was used for grazing horses, Golden Square was first laid out in 1688 shortly after its fashionable neighbour Soho Square. It soon became a popular living area for the gentry. Residents included the 1st Duke of Chandos and the Duchess of Cleveland. In the mid-18th century the square was managed by trustees. In 1753 a statue was erected, which is thought to be by John van Nost depicting George II, but a sign in the square states it is a statue of Charles II. Reputedly it was won by accident at auction when the bidder raised his hand to greet a friend. At the time many of the residents were diplomats, and the painter Angelica Kauffmann lived here from 1767 to 1781. During the next century the neighbourhood declined and instrument makers, boarding houses and small hotels replaced the gentry in the surrounding houses.

During World War II the iron fence was taken for salvage and an air-raid shelter was dug here. Westminster City Council refurbished the square and re-opened it in 1952. Today it features a raised stone terrace with the statue of George II in the centre. The planting consists of geometrical flowerbeds with seasonal plants; a bed with roses donated by the city of Sofia, Bulgaria; pyramid hornbeam (*Carpinus betulus fastigiata*); ornamental crab apple and maple trees. On a fine summer's evening you can see all sorts of people playing table tennis, reading or relaxing. Who knows, someone may break into song any minute, as in Dickens' novel!

Address Golden Square, W1R 3AD, myparks.westminster.gov.uk | **Getting there** Tube to Piccadilly Circus (Piccadilly and Bakerloo Lines) | **Hours** Daily 8am–dusk | **Tip** The Nordic Bakery (37B New Cavendish Street) makes great cinnamon buns!

38 Golders Hill Park
The perfect day out

Adjoining the West Heath and managed by the Corporation of London, Golders Hill Park is technically part of Hampstead Heath but has its own history and definitely its own character.

The majority of the grounds is sloping parkland reputedly landscaped by 'Capability' Brown in the 18th century. The estate and manor house were bought in 1898 by a committee of local residents and turned into a public park in 1899. Today a café stands on the site of the house, which was pulled down in 1940 as it was damaged during the war.

A magnet for children is the small zoo with donkeys, ring-tailed lemurs, ring-tailed coati (named Pedro and Pepe), Patagonian mara, Eurasian eagle owls, laughing kookaburras, white-faced whistling ducks and several other species of birds. There are also a number of fallow deer. Parents will appreciate the fact that the zoo is free – an animal adoption scheme helps to cover the costs, and who wouldn't want to adopt a cute little lemur! Animal lovers can also visit the butterfly house to observe its many British and tropical species. A duck pond with a humpback bridge, a beautifully kept flower garden, a water garden, a swan pond and a bandstand with live music and other events and activities in the summer are further things to explore in this 40-acre green space. Worth visiting also is the recently created 'stumpery' – once a Victorian garden craze – inspired by similar structures at Biddulph Grange Gardens in Staffordshire and the Prince of Wales's stumpery at Highgrove. Here light and shadow play on a path winding down a woodland glade surrounded by ferns, flowers, small streams and tree stumps. A children's play area and sports facilities such as table tennis tables, tennis courts and a croquet lawn provide further entertainment.

It is not surprising that many families spend a whole perfect day in this delightful English landscape garden!

Address West Heath Avenue, NW11 7QP, www.cityoflondon.gov.uk | Getting there Tube to Golders Green (Northern Line) | Hours Daily 7.30am–dusk | Tip The Old Bull & Bush (North End Way) is a large gastropub with an outdoor terrace.

39_Gordon Square Garden
Full of amusement and sense

Bloomsbury became a fashionable neighbourhood in the 18th century. Master builder Thomas Cubitt began building elegant terraces around formal garden squares here in the 1820s, as part of the Bedford Estate, and the sixth Duke of Bedford himself designed the layout of the garden and supervised the planting. He named it after his second wife, Lady Georgiana Gordon.

Gordon Square experienced another heyday when the Bloomsbury Set moved here in the early 20th century. The revitalisation started in 1904, when the Stephen siblings Virginia (Woolf), Vanessa (Bell), Adrian and Thoby moved to 46 Gordon Square. They held their 'Thursday Evenings' here with recitals, conversations and performances of musical numbers and silly plays. Several of their friends followed them to Gordon Square, including Clive Bell, Maynard Keynes, Lytton Strachey and Dora Carrington.

Nowadays the garden belongs to the University of London. After a seven-year restoration project it re-opened in 2007 and is managed to support wildlife. A woodland area under mature plane trees with dog violets, cow parsley and three different types of bluebells encourages birds and butterflies. Some areas are left undisturbed and dense thickets provide nesting sites. Two sculptures have been installed. One of them depicts the poet and philosopher Rabindranath Tagore; the other is a bust of Noor Inayat Khan, an agent who infiltrated occupied France in World War II.

A former gardener's hut turned kiosk sells good coffee and refreshments. In summer the garden is busy, but with a relaxed atmosphere: scented roses flower in a central border, the benches are occupied, students nap, read and chat on the lawn. Lady Gordon, who bore the sixth Duke of Bedford ten children and had several lovers, was once described as 'full of amusement and sense' – a fitting namesake for this beautiful garden!

Address Gordon Square, WC1H 0PQ, www.bloomsburysquares.wordpress.com/
gordon-square | Getting there Tube to Euston Square (Circle, Hammersmith & City,
Metropolitan Lines) | Hours Daily 8am–8pm or dusk, whichever is earlier, closed
on Christmas Day | Tip Walk around Gordon Square and discover exactly where the
'Bloomsberries' lived. The houses are marked by blue plaques.

40 Gray's Inn Gardens
Walks for benchers

Also known as 'The Walks', Gray's Inn Gardens are the largest privately owned gardens in London. Over 400 years old, they have many stories to tell. Around 1660 Samuel Pepys had his eye on pretty promenading ladies as he went 'to Gray's Inn where I saw many beauties'. In 1701 a duel took place here, unfortunately resulting in the death of one of the opponents. And in the 19th century Dickens was employed as a junior clerk in a law office on the premises, working all day at a high desk.

Gray's Inn is one of London's four Inns of Court, professional associations for barristers and judges founded around 700 years ago. Only these four Inns have the right to call people 'to the bar' of England and Wales. In 1606 Sir Francis Bacon, Treasurer at Gray's Inn, presided over the committee that laid out the gardens with their main feature being avenues of trees clipped into shape. Bacon also built a summerhouse and allegedly planted two catalpa trees (*Catalpa bignonioides)*, one of which still stands today. Its trumpet-shaped flowers appear in June and early July. Although the tree looks ancient it is unlikely that Bacon planted it.

Today the sloping 5.8-acre plot is still surrounded by barristers' chambers and offices. It offers mixed planting with a central path lined by American red oaks (*Quercus rubra)*. It also features tall old London planes, a sloping bank planted with wildflowers containing daffodils in spring and oxeye daisies followed by grasses in summer. There are beautiful borders filled with perennials including acanthus, geranium and phlox. Roses, such as the deep red Guinee or the pink-edged Handel, cover the railings, and in June clusters of multicoloured hollyhocks are in flower.

By the way, the term 'bencher' refers to a member of the governing body of the Honourable Society of Gray's Inn, who originally sat on benches in the main hall of the Inn.

Address 8 South Square, WC1R 5ET, www.graysinn.org.uk/the-inn/the-walks | **Getting there** Tube to Chancery Lane (Central Line) | **Hours** Mon–Fri noon–2.30pm, closed on public holidays | **Tip** Visit nearby Leather Lane Street Market (10am–2pm) for good coffee and street food.

41__Green Park

No flowers

The name of the park commonly known as Green Park is entirely fitting, as it is mostly green! In summer, autumn and winter it appears as an expanse of grass and mature trees. This is altogether different for a few weeks in spring when 250,000 daffodil bulbs burst into life and transform the park into a sea of yellow.

This smallest of the Royal Parks unusually has no lake, pond or other body of water – although beneath it flows the Tyburn, a stream running from Hampstead to the Thames. Most of the trees here are lime or plane alternating with more unusual trees such as the native black poplar (*Populus nigra)* and silver lime *(Tilia tomentosa).* The most notable feature is the Broadwalk, which follows the course of the Tyburn, planted in 1905 to frame the view of the Queen Victoria Memorial.

Green Park owes its existence to Charles II, who wanted to walk from Hyde Park to St. James's Park without leaving royal soil. He bought the piece of land between the two parks, built a wall around it and called it Upper St. James's Park, which later became Green Park. He came here for his daily walk, his 'constitutional', which gave Constitution Hill, one of the park's perimeter roads, its name. Throughout the park's history it has seen some dark moments. One of them occurred in 1749 when a big fireworks display took place, to which Handel composed his *Music for the Royal Fireworks.* The temple where the fireworks were stored was hit by a stray rocket; the building exploded and three people died in the ensuing fire. In the 18th century the park became a haunt of highwaymen. An assassination attempt was made here on Queen Victoria and Prince Albert in 1840, but they escaped unscathed.

As to the lack of flower beds: It is said that Charles II's wife caught him picking flowers for his mistress and ordered the removal of all flowers.

Address Constitution Hill, SW1A 1BW, www.royalparks.org.uk/parks/green-park, stjames@royalparks.gsi.gov.uk | **Getting there** Tube to Green Park (Jubilee, Piccadilly and Victoria Lines) | **Hours** Unrestricted | **Tip** Berry Bros. & Rudd is Britain's oldest wine and spirit merchant (3 St James's Street).

42 Greenwich Park

0° 0' 0"

The oldest enclosed Royal Park is a designated World Heritage Site of outstanding universal value. Early stone tools indicate pre-Roman settlements, and the remains of a building, presumably a Romano-Celtic temple, were found in 1902.

Henry VIII was born in Greenwich and married two of his wives here. His daughter Elizabeth I picnicked near a hollow chestnut tree that her parents had danced around. In the early 17th century, King James I reshaped the park. He built a high brick wall around it and gave the park and palace to his wife, Anne – most likely as an apology for swearing at her in public when she accidentally shot his favourite dog. Inigo Jones built the Queen's House (today part of the National Maritime Museum) for her, but she died before it was finished.

In 1662 Charles II commissioned André Le Nôtre to re-landscape the park and started to build a new palace. Neither project was finished because Charles ran out of money. Le Nôtre went on to landscape Versailles. More successful was the Royal Observatory (originally Flamsteed House), which Christopher Wren built for the king.

The palace was demolished and Greenwich Hospital was built, which The Royal Naval College occupied from 1873.

On top of its royal history the 183-acre park offers brilliant views of the Docklands and the City of London. Visit the semi-circular Rose Garden containing hybrid tea and floribunda roses; the Flower Garden and its seasonal beds, cedars and tulip trees; the Herb Garden, planted around a central fountain with a pattern formed by clipped box hedges; the long herbaceous border, re-designed by Chris Beardshaw in 2013; and the Queen's Orchard with heritage fruit trees and a vegetable area.

What more can be asked of a park where East meets West and you can stand on the Prime Meridian of the world? Deer, perhaps? You'll find those too.

Address Greenwich Park, SE10 8XJ, www.royalparks.org.uk/parks/greenwich-park |
Getting there Train to Cutty Sark for Maritime Greenwich (Dockland Light Railway) or
Greenwich (Southeastern) | Hours Daily 6am–sunset | Tip An interesting way to reach
the Isle of Dogs by foot is via the Greenwich Foot Tunnel (the entrance is near the Cutty
Sark), built in 1902 with glazed domes at both ends.

43___Grosvenor Gardens

Uproar in London's French Garden

What do Marshal Foch, a lioness and a kudu antelope have in common? Where do you see shell huts in Central London? And where do women protest? The answers can be found in two small triangular gardens near Victoria Station. Laid out in 1864 to form an ensemble with Thomas Cundy's French Renaissance-style houses, Lower and Upper Grosvenor Gardens remain in the possession of the Duke of Westminster and are leased by Westminster Council.

The Lower Garden gained its current appearance in 1952 when it was redesigned by Jean Moreux, the architect-in-chief of the National Monuments and Palaces of France as a memorial to Anglo-French understanding. He also created the two shell huts decorated with shells from French and English beaches – a truly cross-cultural undertaking. The original fleur-de-lys pattern in the centre was replaced by a low, circular box hedge. An equestrian statue of Marshal Foch stands at the entrance of the park. It was designed by the sculptor Georges Malissard, who insisted it should be placed at the southern end where all the Frenchmen arriving in London could see it. Foch (1851–1929) is the only French military commander to have been made an honorary field marshal in the British Army.

For a long time the Upper Garden was only open to residents. In 1999–2000 the railings were restored and it was re-landscaped with a central lawn and a path around the perimeter. Today its main attraction is a life-size statue of a lioness chasing a lesser kudu, created by Jonathan Kenworthy, which was commissioned by the Duke of Westminster and placed here in 2000.

Grosvenor Gardens was also the place where 20,000 suffragettes started marching for women's rights in 1914. Emmeline Pankhurst led them towards Buckingham Palace to present a petition to the king – and was promptly arrested. Fittingly the women's march in 2016 started in the same location.

Address Grosvenor Gardens, SW1W, myparks.westminster.gov.uk, parks@westminster.gov.uk | **Getting there** Tube to Victoria (Circle, District and Victoria Lines) | **Hours** End of British Summer Time to 15 Feb 10am–4.30pm; 16 Feb to 28/29 Feb 10am–5.30pm; 1 Mar to end of British Summer Time 10am–6pm | **Tip** Discover the collection of royal carriages in the Royal Mews, Buckingham Palace.

44___Hackney City Farm

Hackney's celebrities

If you enjoy celebrity spotting you've come to the right place. Larry is a TV star featured on BBC and ITV. He also takes part in annual nativity parades and Easter events. He enjoys your visit, is very vocal and doesn't mind if you take pictures. He lives at Hackney City Farm… and is a donkey.

And he's not the only one! His companion is called Clover and they're the stars of the farm, which unfortunately makes them a bit fat on too many treats from the visitors. There are also goats, rabbits, chicken, pigs, ducks and sheep, some of whom occasionally go on holiday to a farm in Kent, to give them a bit of time off in the country.

Eggs from the chickens are sold at the farm shop and several beehives provide honey. The cottage garden is filled with flowers and also produces fruit and vegetables, which are often used in the kitchen of the on-site Italian café, Frizzante.

Hackney City Farm was founded in the 1980s by enthusiastic members of the local community who wanted to give children the opportunity to experience farming in the city. Two hundred years ago the site was also farmland, supplying produce to the city. From the 1880s, several businesses – from a brewery to a button manufacturer – occupied the plot until it went back to being a farm in 1984. The old outbuildings in the grounds were turned into stables; offices in containers and a straw-bale building were added. Today the farm also features a well-equipped pottery studio, offers mosaic classes and engages in other community projects such as the creation of an orchard at Haggerston Park. In times of council cutbacks the farm looks for different funding opportunities: providing office workspace to other charities, offering veg box schemes for locals and selling souvenirs and toys. Larry certainly does his bit, as no self-respecting famous donkey would want to live anywhere else than Hackney City Farm!

Address 1a Goldsmiths Row, E2 8QA, www.hackneycityfarm.co.uk,
farm@hackneycityfarm.co.uk | Getting there London Overground to Hoxton
(East London Line) | Hours Tue–Sun 10am–4.30pm | Tip Alternative London
offers walking tours, bike tours and street art workshops (Unit 5, The Yard, Yorkton
Street, www.alternativeldn.co.uk).

45 __ Haggerston Park

Gaslight and Mickey Mouse

For 120 years Haggerston Park was the site of the Gas Light and Coke Company, which provided large parts of London with energy. In the 1930s it produced over five million cubic feet of gas every day. It even had its own stretch of canal where barges could be loaded and unloaded. This all came to an abrupt halt in 1944 when a V2 rocket hit the gasworks. In 1958 the park was opened on the site with the original boundary walls of the gasworks still visible. It had a nautical theme with a bandstand, sundial and clock tower. Further extension in the 1980s included the development of Hackney City Farm (see ch. 44).

Today this open space covers nearly 15 acres of land. A long pergola walk on the north side of the park is entirely covered by a magnificent blue wisteria that bursts into flower in May. Towards the northwest exit a slightly sunken strip of land is planted with tall birch trees, ceanothus bushes and perennials. This is the former canal, which was filled in during the 1950s. There is a beautiful wildlife pond, and 180 volunteers helped to clear the ground and plant 200 plants in a community orchard and food-growing garden. The park is also a sports hub for the community with lots of facilities such as a BMX track, where coaching sessions are offered by Hackney BMX Club; an athletics track (seasonal); a multi-usage games area for tennis, football, basketball and netball; table tennis tables and a trim trail with wooden multi-gym equipment.

The Sebright Children Centre is located in the park and at the moment Hackney Council is planning to build a temporary school on the old parks depot site, which will later be accessible to the public. Several music festivals and events take place in the park each year. And last but not least: Mickey Mouse visited the park in 1992 together with Minnie Mouse and Michael Jackson. They arrived by helicopter to visit a nearby children's hospital.

Address Audrey Street, E2 8QH, www.hackney.gov.uk/haggerston-park,
parks@hackney.gov.uk | Getting there London Overground to Hoxton (East London Line) |
Hours Daily 7.30am–dusk | Tip Try food from Georgia in the Little Georgia Café
(87 Goldsmiths Row).

46 Hampstead Heath

A park for four seasons

In spring the meadows are full of crocuses and daffodils followed by hawthorn blossom and oxeye daisies in the long grass. The joys of summer include swimming in the ponds, open-air concerts and lazy picnics. In autumn people fly kites on Parliament Hill, and winter sees frosty leaves and ice on the ponds. On rare occasions a snowfall leads to a frenzy of imaginative snowman-building.

With 790 acres, Hampstead Heath is not only one of London's biggest open spaces, it is also packed with history, wildlife, sporting facilities and some of the best views over London from Parliament Hill, which supposedly got its name because you can see Parliament from here.

Of the over 500 veteran trees on the Heath, one old beech tree is the particular favourite of North London children, as it is hollow and several children can climb in at the same time.

Most of the many ponds here are man-made, dug in the 17th and 18th centuries to meet London's growing water demands. Today, three of them are used for swimming: the ladies' pond, the men's pond and the mixed pond. Another great feature of the park are the over 16 different sports that are supported here. It is the home of British cross-country running but there is also an athletics track, a lido, tennis courts, a bowling green, a petanque pitch and a volleyball court. Children can switch between eight different play areas including a paddling pool and adventure playground.

Kenwood House and Estate comprise an azalea and rhododendron garden which blooms gloriously in May, two ponds, one fake bridge and the house itself, a neoclassical masterpiece transformed by Robert Adams. It houses an amazing collection of artworks including paintings by Rembrandt and Vermeer. With so much to see and to do it is not enough to visit Hampstead Heath once or twice. You have to come back in all four seasons.

Address East Heath Road, NW3 2SY, www.hampsteadheath.net, enquiries@hampsteadheath.net | Getting there London Overground to Hampstead Heath or Gospel Oak (North London Line); or tube to Hampstead (Northern Line) | Hours Unrestricted | Tip Visit Parliament Hill Farmers Market on a Saturday morning followed by pasta for lunch at Parliament Hill Café.

47__Hampton Court Palace
Everything a king could need

Even the deer have a royal history here: the 300 fallow deer on the estate are all descended from Henry VIII's original herd. The palace and gardens became royal when Henry's first minister Cardinal Wolsey fell from favour in 1529, and the king made it his own and created a showpiece of English gardening. So, just imagine for a moment that you were king or queen and had to choose between these features:

The oldest surviving hedge maze in the United Kingdom. It was planted in 1702 with half a mile of winding paths. It takes around 20 minutes to get to the centre. How long will it take you to get out?

Dessert grapes for your table. The world's oldest and largest grapevine was planted by 'Capability' Brown in 1768 and still produces grapes in its own greenhouse that are sold in the palace shops.

No king can go without a great parterre or fountain garden. These were designed by Daniel Marot with a glistening fountain and yew trees clipped into giant umbrella shapes.

Your own privy garden. This one was created for William III in 1702 with a formal parterre, marble sculptures and large wrought-iron screens by Jean Tijou.

Of course, you need a kitchen garden as well. This one includes seasonal fruits, vegetables and herbs that would have served the Georgian kings in the 18th century.

A rose garden, pond gardens, wilderness with daffodils in spring, a 20th century garden, 15 glasshouses and three National Plant Collections: Heliotropium, Lantana and Queen Mary II's Exoticks are thrown in for good measure.

There is no choice; you have to have all of them. By the way, you'll need 42 gardeners to look after your 60 acres of formal gardens and 750 acres of royal parkland.

Are you still keen on being a queen or king? Or would you rather buy a ticket and feel royal for just a day?

Address Hampton Court Palace, East Molesey, KT8 9AU, +44 (0)20 3166 6000, www.hrp.org.uk, hamptoncourt@hrp.org.uk | Getting there Train to Hampton Court (South West Trains) | Hours 30 Oct–25 March 10am–4.30pm; 26 March–28 Oct 10am–6pm | Tip Go back to London on the Thames. Hampton Court has its own riverboat stop (www.wpsa.co.uk).

48 Highgate Cemetery
Monumental

Opened in 1839, Highgate Cemetery is one of the 'magnificent seven' private cemeteries that were created to solve the shortage of burial grounds in Central London. The Grade I listed cemetery is probably the most iconic. With its mixture of architectural styles it is a Victorian burial fantasy come true. The architect behind this 'monumental enterprise' is the founder of the London Cemetery Company, Stephen Geary, who designed the unique structure together with James Bunstone Bunning, and David Ramsay as landscape architect.

The older West Cemetery comprises the majority of the architectural highlights, starting with the two Tudor Revival style chapels with wooden turrets and a bell tower that also forms an archway over the entrance. One of the most impressive structures is the Egyptian Avenue with an arched entrance flanked by Egyptian-style columns. The vaults in the Circle of Lebanon are topped by a cedar of Lebanon, which predates the cemetery. The East Cemetery on the other side of Swain's Lane is much more restrained in its architectural grandeur. Here, nature has taken over (the cemetery is also a nature reserve). Imposing trees tower over bluebell carpets in spring and ivy and wild roses cover the leaning gravestones, suggesting an enchanted forest rather than a graveyard.

Another attraction is the diversity of interesting people buried here. Among them are the writers George Eliot and Douglas Adams, the painter Lucian Freud, the family of Charles Dickens and the scientist Michael Faraday. The most famous is easily Karl Marx but only around ten mourners attended his funeral in 1883 – in comparison the funeral of the bare-knuckled prize-fighter Tom Sayers, with his dog as chief mourner, attracted more than 10,000. Highgate Cemetery inspired several novels and films and even has its own supernatural apparition, the Highgate Vampire.

Address Swain's Lane, N6 6PJ, www.highgatecemetery.org, info@highgatecemetery.org | Getting there Tube to Archway (Northern Line) | Hours East Cemetery: Mon–Fri 10am–5pm, Sat, Sun & public holidays 11am–5pm; West Cemetery: by guided tour only, check website for further information. | Tip Highgate Literary & Scientific Institution (www.hlsi.net) offers weekly lectures, film screenings, art exhibitions and musical events.

49 __ Highgate Wood
Walk back through time

This 70-acre piece of land has been woodland for many hundreds of years, and is classified as one of four ancient woodlands in the London borough of Haringey (the others are Queen's Wood, Coldfall Wood and Bluebell Wood). The rich diversity of wildlife here – 900 species of invertebrate, 338 moth species, 353 different fungi, 70 bird species and 7 bat species – is the result of very careful management, coppicing certain trees while leaving others to mature, encouraging regeneration and creating diverse habitats.

Ancient woodlands are those that predate 1600, and are the result of interaction between humans and nature. For many centuries these places supplied wood for fuel, house and shipbuilding. Traces of this interaction can be found everywhere in Highgate Wood. The predominant tree species here are oak and hornbeam. Some of the ancient hornbeam trees have fused together, an old woodland management technique where several saplings were planted in one hole to grow more timber. Many old trees are coppiced, others pollarded, and you can see the remains of layered hedges. You can also find the wild service tree (*Sorbus torminalis*), an indicator of ancient woodland.

Other historic remnants are ancient earthworks running through the wood. Mesolithic flint tools, arrows and blades have been found, indicating that people hunted here. Later the Romans built a pottery factory, and in the 13th century the wood became a hunting park for the Bishops of London. In the 19th century it was known as Gravel Pit Wood as gravel was extracted from the west side of the area. In 1886, when it became a public park, many trees were felled, paths were cleared and a Tudor-style lodge was built. A drinking fountain was erected in memory of Samuel Taylor Coleridge, who supposedly liked to walk here. Highgate Wood's journey through time hopefully will continue for many years to come.

Address Muswell Hill Road, N6, www.cityoflondon.gov.uk/things-to-do/green-spaces | Getting there Tube to Highgate (Northern Line) | Hours Daily 7.30am – dusk | Tip Continue your walk in neighbouring Queen's Wood. Like Highgate Wood, it was originally part of the ancient Forest of Middlesex.

50__Hill Garden and Pergola
A dream garden

This Edwardian extravaganza is a nearly 250-metre-long raised brick walk and pergola, where paired Doric stone columns, wooden beams and countless climbers create an ever-changing display of light and shadow. Although it officially belongs to Hampstead Heath, a road separates the two.

You can access the pergola from North End Way via a path to the left of Inverforth House (formerly The Hill). Open a wooden door at its base and climb the spiral staircase. The raised walkway of the pergola stands about 15 feet above the ground. Here climbing roses, honeysuckle, jasmine, clematis and kiwi plants wind up the columns. On one side you can see Inverforth House with its terraced garden; on the other is the restored formal kitchen garden with aromatic herbs, perennials and espalier apple trees. Cross a stone bridge over a footpath and look down on a little box parterre and the Hill Garden with its ornamental lily pond and mature shrubs and trees. There is a belvedere and a little summerhouse at the end of the walk with views over the West Heath.

This dreamy place was created by the soap manufacturer and philanthropist William Hesketh Lever, later Lord Leverhulme, who bought the 19th century manor Hill House in 1904, renamed it The Hill and commissioned Thomas Mawson to create his dream garden. The pergola was built in three stages between 1906 and 1925. Lots of spoil was needed to raise the garden. Luckily the Hampstead part of the Northern Line was being built at the time and the contractors needed a place to dump the spoil. In the end Leverhulme even managed to get paid a nominal fee for receiving the material he needed for his garden.

A major refurbishment in 1995 restored the garden's Edwardian splendour. Lord Leverhulme's dream garden is still one of London's less known gardens, but has become a romantic destination for proposals and wedding photos.

Address Inverforth Close, NW3 7EX, www.cityoflondon.gov.uk | **Getting there** Tube to Golders Green (Northern Line) | **Hours** Daily dawn–dusk | **Tip** Walk to Whitestone Pond, the pedestrian hub between the West Heath and Hampstead Heath. It is the highest point in London!

51 __ Holland Park
A Victorian garden party

This 55-acre park is the largest green space in the Borough of Kensington and Chelsea. In the 17th century it was part of a 500-acre estate that surrounded Cope Castle, a Jacobean mansion built for Sir Walter Cope. Later it became Holland House, named after the Earl of Holland, whose wife was the first Englishwoman to successfully grow dahlias. In the 19th century parts of the estate were sold for housing development, and bombs destroyed most of Holland House in 1940.

The park opened to the public in 1952. It comprises an arboretum and areas of woodland with glades full of foxgloves. In order to manage the wildflower meadows, cows were used in recent years to graze them. The playground provides entertainment for families with children with its giant see-saw, tyre swing and zip wire. There are facilities for cricket, football, tennis, golf and squash. A theatre in the park and the Ice House built for the Holland Estate and turned into exhibition space provide entertainment for the culturally minded.

Two of the park's highlights are the Acer Avenue and the Kyoto Garden, both especially beautiful in autumn when the trees change colour to every shade of red and yellow. The Kyoto Garden was designed by Shoji Nakahara on the occasion of the Japan Festival in 1992. It is surrounded by bamboo fencing and features a waterfall, a bridge and a koi pond. Here and everywhere else in the park you can see peacocks strutting around and showing off their colourful plumage. Some of the formal estate gardens were preserved, including the Dutch Garden, today home to Lady Holland's dahlia collection.

This park invites visitors to stroll. Its atmosphere is best caught in a mural in the Orangery Arcade by the artist Mao Wenbiao depicting an imagined garden party here in the 1870s, which will transport you straight back to a Victorian summer's day.

Address Ilchester Place, W8, www.rbkc.gov.uk/leisure-and-culture/parks/holland-park |
Getting there Tube to High Street Kensington (Circle and District Lines) | **Hours** Daily
7.30am – 30 minutes before sunset | **Tip** When is a park not a park? When it's an opera!
Opera Holland Park offers world-class opera and rain-protected picnic areas in the summer.

52 Horniman Museum

Indoors and outdoors

Fred Horniman (1835-1906) was a very successful tea merchant, the first to use machine-sealed packaging. On his travels around the world he started collecting objects, specimens and artefacts that soon filled his house to the brim. It became too much for his wife, who told him that 'either the collection goes or we do'.

The family moved out and the museum opened in their former residence in 1895. After the collection grew even further, Horniman rebuilt the museum and gifted it to the people in 1901 for their 'recreation, instruction and enjoyment'. He requested that the museum and the gardens should be treated as a unity and this request has been the guideline for designing and managing the garden until today, with amazing results.

The over-16-acre site contains display gardens created to link the indoor and outdoor collections such as the Sound Garden. It is great fun to play the oversized Spiral Scraper, Bat Pipes or the Chime Run, instruments that are also part of the musical instrument collection in the museum. The Medicinal Garden is planted in 'body part' sections and tells you all about the plants used to treat diseases of these parts. The Dye Garden features plants that give us colours and explains the processes to produce them. The Animal Walk with live alpaca, goats, sheep and chicken looks at the differences between domesticated animals and their wild relatives, and the Prehistoric Garden contains 'living fossils', plants that evolved 360 million years ago and are still around today.

Anyone who still has leftover energy can visit the beautiful Grade II listed conservatory, totem pole, sundials, nature trail, wildlife garden, bandstand and several other things you shouldn't miss. Or just sit down on a bench and enjoy the vistas of London. You will have to come back anyway because the amazing indoor collections are still waiting to be seen.

Address 100 London Road, SE23 3PQ, +44 (0)20 8699 1872, www.horniman.ac.uk, enquiry@horniman.ac.uk | Getting there London Overground to Forest Hill (East London Line) | Hours Mon–Sat 7.15am–sunset; Sun 8am–sunset | Tip Stag & Bow is a very nice haberdashery shop where you can also learn how to knit, crochet and do all kinds of crafts (8 Dartmouth Road).

53_Hyde Park
Favourite thing to do?

How can you answer that, when you are as spoilt for choice as visitors are in Hyde Park?

As were many of the Royal Parks, this park was once a hunting ground for Henry VIII, and opened to the public for the first time in 1637. When Britain's upper classes wanted to see and to be seen in the 18th century, they went horse riding on Rotten Row, a riding path created by William III in 1690, originally named 'Route du Roi'. William also installed 300 oil lamps here, the first street lighting in England, supposedly to deter highwaymen. You can still go riding on Rotten Row with fewer highwaymen to fear, and a special traffic light for horse riders instead.

What to enjoy next? Proceed to the Serpentine Lake where you can rent a boat or go swimming in the lido, both activities that were already popular here in the 19th century. You can also watch cormorants, great crested grebes with their elaborate mating display, and bats that fly at dusk. On the park roads people are cycling, roller-blading or skateboarding; join in or do the opposite and rent a green and white striped deckchair to relax for a few hours. If you are politically minded you can listen to the orators at Speakers' Corner or stand on a soapbox yourself and exercise your right to speak.

Another favourite activity could be to visit the park's monuments. Some of the most interesting are the 7 July Memorial that commemorates the victims of the London bombings of 2005, the Diana Memorial Fountain with its serene flowing water and the Wellington Monument made from canons the Duke of Wellington captured in France. It depicts an 18-foot-high nude Achilles and was London's first nude statue since antiquity and caused outrage when it was installed in 1822. Laurence Olivier said that it had 'the best arse in London'.

Have you done all that? Now, what is your favourite thing to do in Hyde Park?

Address Hyde Park Corner, SW1X 7LY, www.royalparks.org.uk/parks/hyde-park | Getting there Tube to Hyde Park Corner (Piccadilly Line) or Marble Arch (Central Line) | Hours Daily 5am–midnight | Tip If you want to know more about the Duke of Wellington visit his former home, Apsley House, which also houses a fine art collection (149 Piccadilly, Hyde Park Corner).

54 Inner Temple Garden

The first brawl of the Wars of the Roses?

…at least according to Shakespeare. In his play *Henry VI*, he set the dispute between Richard Plantagenet and John Beaufort that led to the Wars of the Roses in the Inner Temple Garden: 'And here I prophesy: this brawl to-day, / Grown to this faction in the Temple-garden, / Shall send between the red rose and the white / A thousand souls to death and deadly night.'

Already in Shakespeare's time the garden was known for its beautiful roses, but it goes back much further, to 1160, when the Knights Templar settled here. In 1608 James I granted the land to 'the students and practitioners of the laws of the realm' and it has belonged ever since to the benchers of the Inner Temple and Middle Temple, two of the four Inns of Court.

Later the garden was remodelled in the Dutch style and the 18th and 19th centuries saw an enlargement of the garden and the planting of the double row of planes. Its direct access to the Thames was lost after Bazelgatte constructed the Victoria Embankment.

Today much of the garden alludes to its long history. Several large fruit trees such as a black mulberry, a quince, a medlar and a walnut acknowledge the garden's history as an orchard in medieval times, and a bed has been planted with roses to commemorate the Shakespeare connection.

The beauty of the herbaceous borders that flower profusely for the majority of the year are the work of head gardener Andrea Brunsendorf and her team, who undertook some major regeneration and replanting. The High Border enchants in spring with forget-me-nots, tulips and wallflowers, followed by aquilegias and alliums. Peonies and wisteria are in bloom in May and June in the Peony Garden. In other borders shrub roses are underplanted with lady's mantle and catmint, and in August blowsy hydrangeas and lilies take centre stage. This garden is far too beautiful to start wars in, even if they are 'wars of the roses'.

Address Crown Office Row, EC4Y 7HL, www.innertemple.org.uk | Getting there Tube to Temple (Circle and District Lines) | Hours Mon–Fri 12.30pm–3pm | Tip There are several courtyards in the Inner Temple precinct that have small landscaped gardens worth looking at, among them the Church Court, Pump Court and Elm Court.

55__Kennington Park

Life is beautiful…

…so enjoy it to the fullest! These words are printed on a small sign in Kennington Park Flower Garden, and can be endorsed wholeheartedly, especially in regard to Kennington Park's eventful history. Its predecessor was Kennington Common, where cricket was played in the early 18th century but which was also used for public executions. The Methodists John Wesley and George Whitefield preached here in 1739 and in the 19th century thousands of Chartists gathered here calling for electoral reforms. The Prince Consort's lodge, a 'model dwelling' commissioned by Prince Albert and built for the Great Exhibition of 1851 to demonstrate efficient accommodation at low cost, was moved here in 1853. In 1854 the common was turned into a public park, the first of its kind in Lambeth. It was laid out with a central lawn with perimeter paths lined by plane trees. It also contains two ornamental drinking fountains and an art deco teahouse.

During both world wars the park was bombed; in World War II a public air-raid shelter was hit and 104 people died. Some parts were turned into allotments. Today it is a multi-purpose green space with sport facilities and playgrounds, much loved by the locals. But the park's jewel is the Kennington Park Flower Garden or Old English Garden. Opened in 1931, the formal garden with a pergola and rose and perennial beds was created to resemble the designs of Colonel J J Sexby, who created a number of South London parks. The garden fell into disrepair until Lambeth Council and Friends of Kennington Park joined forces to restore the site, and re-opened in 2015. Come here on a sunny spring day to see the jewel-coloured tulips, nearly transparent white narcissi interspersed with flowing grasses and the magnificent *Fritillaria imperialis*. Sit on a bench and watch the blue tits nipping at seeds in the bird feeder. Isn't life beautiful?

Address Kennington Park Road, SE11 4BE, www.kenningtonpark.org, info@kenningtonpark.org | **Getting there** Tube to Oval (Central Line) | **Hours** Daily 7.30am – 15 minutes before sunset | **Tip** Ovalhouse Theatre showcases radical new theatre productions (52 – 54 Kennington Oval, www.ovalhouse.com).

56 Kensal Green Cemetery

Greener than Père-Lachaise

In the 19th century, London's population more than doubled, leading to overcrowded parish churchyards and disease. A bill was passed to establish large private cemeteries outside of London, and in the next 10 years the 'magnificent seven' were created. Kensal Green Cemetery was the first to open its gates, in 1833, and was built by the General Cemetery Company that still owns and manages the 72-acre site today. The company wanted to create 'a place of recreation that would be morally uplifting and edifying to the general populace'. John Griffith designed the main buildings such as the Dissenters' Chapel and the Anglican Chapel and three catacombs in the neoclassical style. The landscape designs were by Richard Forrest, a former head gardener at Syon Park.

The formal avenues combined with densely planted trees, shrubs, evergreens and flowers were probably inspired by Père-Lachaise Cemetery in Paris. Another novelty was the introduction of a dedicated burial space for dissenters while most of the grounds were still consecrated by the Church of England.

Kensal Green was fashionable from the start. The Duke of Sussex and his nephew were interred here as well as many prominent figures such as the authors Wilkie Collins, Anthony Trollope and William Makepeace Thackeray; the mathematician Charles Babbage and the sculptor Eric Gill. Others include the first man to cross Australia from south to north and the last man to fight a duel in England.

There are 140 listed buildings and monuments, catering to every taste and fashion, ranging from Gothic extravaganza to broken-down circus horse. The Memorial Gardens with individually accessible rose bushes are located near the West London Crematorium (where Freddie Mercury was cremated). For all its monuments in stone and marble, Kensal Green Cemetery is a beautiful green space, 'a place of recreation' with a wealth of wildlife.

Address Harrow Road, W10 4RA, www.kensalgreencemetery.com,
enquiries@kensalgreencemetery.com | Getting there Tube to Kensal Green (Bakerloo
Line) | Hours 1 April–30 Sep Mon–Sat 9am–6pm, Sun 10am–6pm; 1 Oct–31 March
Mon–Sat 9am–5pm, Sun 10am–5pm; bank holidays 10am–1pm | Tip Paradise by the
Way of Kensal Green (19 Kilburn Lane) is a vintage-style gastropub with a British menu.

57 __ Kensington Gardens
Feed the birds

Never mind the Albert Memorial, Italian Gardens, Peter Pan Statue, Serpentine Galleries or Kensington Palace. Forget also 265 acres of parkland, majestic trees and ornamental flower beds. Just follow Mary Poppins' advice and feed the birds! Here, in Kensington Gardens, you can get parakeets and blue tits to eat out of your hands.

As you are here already, you might as well also have a look at the Albert Memorial. In all its golden splendour it is one of London's most ornate monuments and was designed by George Gilbert Scott. Queen Victoria wanted to commemorate her beloved husband with a fitting monument and she herself approved the design, which shows Albert holding a catalogue of the Great Exhibition of 1851, which he initiated.

There is also *The Arch*, a sculpture by Henry Moore that can hardly be missed as it stands six metres tall, and is made of luminous Roman travertine.

If you are here with children you have to visit the Diana, Princess of Wales Memorial Playground, which is a pirate ship – and next to it the Elfin Oak, a hollow oak with figures of fairies, elves and animals peeking out of every nook and cranny.

Actually, the Italian Gardens are worth visiting too. Prince Albert is said to have given them to Victoria and their initials can be seen on a wall on the pump house. Located at the head of the Long Waters, the gardens were designed by James Pennethorne and consist of four basins with urns, statues, dolphins and a fountain.

Kensington Palace itself has some beautiful gardens, especially the Sunken Garden, a formal garden with classic proportions and bright colours. The Serpentine Galleries need their own visit with a great programme of contemporary art and architecture exhibitions.

These are only a few detours. Now you should get back to your main task: get some seeds to feed the birds!

Address Kensington High Street, W2 2UH, www.royalparks.org.uk/parks, kensington@royalparks.gsi.gov.uk | Getting there Tube to High Street Kensington (Circle and District Lines) | Hours Daily 6am–dusk | Tip After a walk in the park you can refresh yourself with traditional afternoon tea in the Orangery Restaurant next to Kensington Palace.

58 Kensington Memorial Park

The best way to remember

Originally called St Mark's Park, and part of the St Quintin Estate in North Kensington, Kensington Memorial Park was developed as farmland from the 1860s. In 1923 the Kensington War Memorial Committee, which had found that creating a new recreational space was the ideal way to remember those who had given their lives in World War I, bought the land for the sum of £8,800. The London County Council laid out the space, mainly as a children's playground as the area had nearly no play spaces for children. Princess Louise, Duchess of Argyll opened Kensington Memorial Park in 1926.

The main attraction of the park is its water-play feature, which is open from May to September. This is not merely a paddling pool but a fully fledged water-play area with sprinklers and fountains and everything imaginable to get you wet, which is a blessing for urban children (and perhaps parents too?) on a hot day. The playground with a sandpit and space rocket climbing frames is also very popular. There is a 'one o'clock club' for children under five and sports facilities for tennis, football and junior cricket. A small kiosk provides snacks and refreshments during the summer – and there is even a dog toilet.

A row of tall Lombardy poplars gives the park a light and airy feel and there's a surprise waiting around the corner in the form of a beautifully planted and well-maintained formal garden with a small pergola, circular beds of perennials, a central palm tree and a circular stone feature containing lavender and an olive tree.

Prince William, who is the president of the Fields in Trust initiative to commemorate the fallen British soldiers of World War I, visited the park in 2016. He unveiled a plaque and rededicated Kensington Memorial Gardens as a place of public remembrance. What better way is there to remember the dead than with this park dedicated to children?

Address St Mark's Road, W10, www.rbkc.gov.uk/leisure-and-culture/parks/kensington-memorial-park | Getting there Tube to Ladbroke Grove (Circle and Hammersmith & City Lines) | Hours Daily 7.30am – dusk | Tip Just across St Mark's Road is the Carmelite Monastery, where nuns live a mostly silent life, without radio or TV. Check out their website, where you can buy 'crafty nuns' (carmelitesnottinghill.org.uk).

59 Kensington Roof Gardens
Castle in the air

The oldest and maybe the craziest roof garden in London can be found on top of the former Derry & Toms department store on Kensington High Street. Looking up from the street you can just catch a glimpse of green.

The entrance on Derry Street is marked '99 Kensington High Street'. Take the lift to the top floor and enter the fairy-tale gardens conceived by Trevor Bowen, managing director of the Barkers department store. He had seen the gardens at Rockefeller Center in New York and commissioned the Welsh landscape architect Ralph Hancock, who had built them, to do something similar here. When the gardens opened in 1938 they had cost £25,000 to create. Visitors were charged one shilling to enter, which was donated to local charities. Today the gardens, a two-storey clubhouse hosting private events and the Babylon restaurant also on the roof belong to Sir Richard Branson.

The original layout hasn't changed much since 1938. Porthole windows set in the brick walls frame views of the surrounding city. The 6,000-square-metre plot contains three gardens. The main feature of the Spanish Garden is a Moorish-style bell tower set off by vibrant borders and olive and cypress trees. The Tudor Garden consists of three interconnecting courtyards surrounded by red brick walls. Climbing roses cover the Tudor-style arches and barley-twist columns. The English Woodland Garden is particularly pretty in spring with thousands of bulbs including snowdrops, bluebells and muscari. Some of the original trees planted here survive until today and have reached impressive heights considering they grow in only 18 inches of soil. The illusion of a secluded woodland glade with a small bridge and a stream would be complete were it not for four flamingos standing in the pond! Watch them from the restaurant, or sit in one of the Tudor-style courtyards and pretend to be in a castle.

Address 99 Kensington High Street, W8 5SA, +44 (0)20 7937 7994, www.virginlimitededition.com/en/the-roof-gardens | Getting there Tube to High Street Kensington (District and Circle Lines) | Hours Phone ahead to visit the gardens as they are often closed for private events. | Tip Visit nearby Royal Albert Hall, Britain's famous concert venue. They also offer tours (www.royalalberthall.com).

60 Kentish Town City Farm

A surprise for commuters

This is the old-timer among London city farms, set up in 1972 by the community organisation Inter-Action, who rented a cottage with some land that was once a timber yard called Gloster Parquet. There were stables, a workshop and a storehouse, and Inter-Action had the idea to turn the site into a riding school for local children. The farm developed from there and is today supported by the Borough of Camden and the City of London Corporation's charity City Bridge Trust.

The four-acre farm runs along railway lines and contains pasture areas for the animals, a wildlife pond, a riding arena and community gardens. The narrow plot widens to the back where the pond, most of the community gardens and the riding arena are located. The animals include goats – very popular because they love to be stroked – sheep, horses, ducks, chicken, a pig and a cow. The farm's breeding programme leads to lots of cute baby animals in spring.

There are always local kids here helping with the farm work, feeding the animals, riding and grooming the horses. One of the farm's strengths is its educational programme helping disadvantaged children and young people with special needs. The staff offers work experience, job training, play schemes, holiday activities, pony rides and riding therapy. Children in Kentish Town and Gospel Oak have grown up visiting the farm. They often come every day, forge friendships here and the animals and staff sometimes help them to cope with difficult situations they experience in school or at home. Many of them come back to volunteer, others bring their children back. With its sloping grounds and the railway tracks on two sides, Kentish Town City Farm is probably one of the most urban city farms in London. Nevertheless it is much loved and supported by the local community, and commuters new to North London can enjoy the surprise of a cow grazing next to the railway.

Address 1 Cressfield Close, NW5 4BN, www.ktcityfarm.org.uk | Getting there London Overground to Gospel Oak (North London Line) | Hours Daily 9am–5pm | Tip Visit nearby Queen's Crescent market, one of London's oldest markets, for food, household products and discounted clothing (Thu & Sat 9am–3pm).

61 King George's Park

Great for families, not for snakes

The best time to visit here is on an equally sunny and breezy early spring day. Stand on the main north-south path and wait for the wind to pick up: thousands of pink petals will rain down on you from the cherry trees lining the path!

This 55-acre park was created by Arts and Crafts garden designer Percy Cane, who won gold medals for his gardens at the Chelsea Flower Show and also owned two horticultural magazines. King George V, after whom it was named, opened it in 1923. The Wandsworth Open Air Pool, built by the architect Ernest J. Elford in 1939, was a popular addition. The pool changed hands several times over the following decades and closed in 1993, to be replaced by an indoor tennis and bowls centre.

Visitors enter through ornamental gates at the northern end. The nearby pond features a fountain and is crossed by a stone footbridge. Reeds grow near its shore, providing a nesting zone for coots and other waterfowl. Next to it are several poplars, a heather garden and a rockery. There is also a lime tree avenue, and the formal rose garden with a brick pergola comes into its own in early summer. The River Wandle flows partly along its eastern boundary and an adjacent wildlife area provides foraging and shelter for small birds and mammals. The Wandle Trail (see ch. 106) also runs through the park.

Three children's play areas including an adventure playground and a small menagerie attract families but there is also a lot to enjoy for sports enthusiasts, including several tennis courts, trim trails, games pitches and a bowling green.

It is obvious why families like this park, and parents pushing buggies are a very common sight on Cherry Tree Walk, but nobody knows what the five-foot carpet python wanted in the park when she slithered along the edge of a fence in August 2015. In the end she was captured by police officers but no owner could be found.

Address Buckhold Road, SW18 4GB, www.wandsworth.gov.uk/directory_record/552346/king_georges_park | **Getting there** Tube to Southfields (District Line) | **Hours** Daily 8am–dusk | **Tip** At nearby Southside Shopping Centre you can get everything you need for a picnic in the park.

62 Lincoln's Inn Fields

No dancing allowed

This park spreads over seven acres in the urban district of Holborn and is London's largest garden square and the oldest in Camden. The current layout of Lincoln's Inn Fields was implemented in the early 19th century with a cruciform path and a central octagonal pavilion. Lawns with scattered trees and perimeter shrubs screen the park from traffic. The park also features flowerbeds and several sculptures, among them a bust of the surgeon John Hunter; a monument to Margaret MacDonald, wife of the social reformer Ramsay MacDonald and *Camdonian*, a 1980 abstract sculpture by Barry Flanagan.

In spring several ornamental cherries flower beautifully in the square. On a nice summer's day the square is filled with students, office workers and lawyers from the surrounding institutions, and the popping noises of tennis balls from the park's three tennis courts provide a soothing rhythm for people lounging on the lawns or having a quick walk around the square in their lunch break.

In the 17th century this picture would have looked more disturbing. At the time the square, laid out by Inigo Jones, was the site of public executions and duels. By 1659, the land was populated by shady characters called 'Mumpers' and 'Rufflers', idle vagrants and beggars. Games of hazard were played during the day and people were robbed at night.

This only ended in 1735 when money was raised by a tax on the area inhabitants for enclosing the park with railings. It was closed to the public until 1894, when the London County Council leased the Fields from Lincoln's Inn, the freeholder of the property, for £12,000. The trustees put up some provisions to protect the quiet, studious nature of a legal and learning environment, which are still in place today. For instance, no noisy games, exhibitions, shows or dancing are allowed in the park at all. Are your feet itching already?

Address Lincoln's Inn Fields, WC2A 3TL, www.camden.gov.uk/ccm/content/leisure/ outdoor-camden/great-parks-in-camden | Getting there Tube to Holborn (Central and Piccadilly Lines) | Hours Daily 7.30–dusk | Tip One of the most beautiful museums in London is the nearby Soane's Museum, the former house of the architect and collector Sir John Soane, which is unchanged since he died in 1837 (13 Lincoln's Inn Fields).

63 __ Lloyd Park
Knights of Walthamstow

Even when it's raining so much that the ducks find it too wet, Lloyd Park in Walthamstow is still worth visiting, not least because the Georgian mansion in the park houses the William Morris Gallery and illustrates the life and work of its most famous resident, Arts and Crafts designer William Morris. The house (formerly Water House) was Morris' childhood home from 1848 to 1856. It's easy to imagine him sitting in a window seat, looking out on the rainy park and writing poems. Eventually it will cease to rain and you can follow his footsteps outside.

Morris played with his brothers and friends by the moat, which is thought to have been here since medieval times. He dressed up as a knight and saved his friends held captive on the island by an imagined dragon.

Today's park owes its existence less to heroic deeds than to bloodthirsty melodramas. Water House was bought by Edward Lloyd, who made his fortune selling cheap, sensational 'penny dreadful' stories, but subsequently became one of the most successful newspaper publishers in Victorian England. His son Frank gifted the house and grounds to Walthamstow Urban District Council, which opened the park in 1900. Ten more acres were purchased from the Aveling Park Estate, bringing the park to its current size of over 30 acres. Lloyd Park features beautiful old trees such as a large Judas tree *(Cercis siliquastrum)* and several light green cypresses. In 1996 the Tapestry Tree Trail was planted with all the trees Morris mentioned in his poem 'Tapestry Trees'. In 2011-2012 the park was re-landscaped and many of its facilities renewed. A new bridge spans the moat and a William Morris Garden was created on the site of a former sensory garden for the blind. Local residents have always loved the park, whose modern knights are the members of the Green Gym, which combines gardening, fitness activities and work for the community.

Address Forest Road, E17 5EH, www.walthamforest.gov.uk/content/lloyd-park, christopher.patterson@walthamforest.gov.uk | **Getting there** Tube to Walthamstow Central (Victoria Line) | **Hours** Mon–Sat from 8.30am; Sun from 9am; please check website | **Tip** Have a beer at Ye Olde Rose & Crown (53–55 Hoe Street). It also has a studio theatre upstairs.

64 Lucas Gardens

History in Camberwell

Often described as a small Victorian park, Lucas Gardens seems to be just one of many South London green spaces, but it has a peculiar history.

The gardens once belonged to a terrace of 12 Georgian houses. In 1846 Camberwell House Lunatic Asylum opened here, despite local protests, and the gardens became part of its 20-acre grounds. The main part was laid out as a park but it also contained a vegetable patch tended by the inhabitants, a tennis court, putting green and cricket pitch. The patients were encouraged to exercise. Unusually for the time, male and female inmates were allowed to mingle in the garden. These sound like ideal conditions for the patients, most of them paupers, but they might beg to differ, considering the prolonged immersion baths, shock treatment and modified insulin treatment they received.

The hospital was closed in 1955 and Lucas Gardens became a public park, named after James Lucas, then mayor of Camberwell. The very attractive main gates, which were added in the late 20th century, spell out its name in golden letters. Beyond it reside a half-circle bench, a water feature and a raised ornamental flowerbed. From this vantage point the garden looks like nothing more than a long narrow plot, but if you venture further it widens to a much larger green space including mature trees such as cherry, lime, horse chestnut, holm oak and tulip, and is in all about four acres.

In spring the park bursts into flower with flowering shrubs and trees, bluebells, tulips and many bedding plants. You can see people reading books, neighbours chatting, dog owners exercising their pooches and students from nearby Camberwell College of Arts sunbathing. A playground provides welcome entertainment for parents with toddlers. Today the gardens not only represent a piece of history in Camberwell, they also offer locals a wonderful green space to enjoy.

Address Peckham Road, SE5 8PX, www.parksandgardens.org/places-and-people | **Getting there** London Overground (South London Line) or train to Peckham Rye (Thameslink) then bus 12 to Vestry Road | **Hours** Daily 7.30am – sunset | **Tip** The nearby London Stained Glass Company produces amazing traditional and modern stained-glass windows (4K Vanguard Court, www.londonstainedglass.co.uk).

65 Mint Street Park

Putting down roots

As do many city gardens, Mint Street Park in Southwark has a story to tell. It was once the site of a parish workhouse belonging to St George the Martyr in Borough High Street. In 1731 it housed 68 men, women and children. They had to spin yarn and knit stockings, and the children were taught to read and recite the catechism. The workhouse was replaced with a newer, bigger building in 1782. Despite appalling conditions the institution was in use until 1920.

To the west of the workhouse, the Evelina Children's Hospital was built in 1869 by Baron Ferdinand de Rothschild, following a tragic accident in which he lost his wife, Evelina, and their unborn son. The hospital closed as an independent institution in 1976 and was demolished by the end of the 20th century. The site became an open space, which soon gained a reputation for crime and anti-social behaviour. Finally the Bankside Open Spaces Trust (BOST) took over and transformed the park with the help of local volunteers, who use the park daily. Today it contains a community stage, an adventure playground, a football pitch and an outdoor gym.

Many who come across this little park wonder at the beautiful planted borders that are filled with roses, evergreen herbs such as rosemary, lavender and santolina and flowering perennials. Small paths bisecting the beds allow visitors to admire the flowers in all their glory. Woodland areas with stacks of logs that harbour a variety of insects can be found under the trees that form the back of the borders. In late summer *Verbena bonariensis* dominates here, complementing the silvery green of the herbs with cool purple. The planting is created and maintained by people from Putting Down Roots, a gardening project of St Mungo's Hostel, where homeless people can develop a variety of gardening skills. In this small park not only the plants are putting down roots.

Address Southwark Bridge Road/Marshalsea Road, SE1 1QX, www.bost.org.uk/
open-places/mint-street-park | Getting there Tube to Borough (Northern Line) |
Hours Unrestricted | Tip Not far from here you can visit the opposite of a garden:
The Shard, London's iconic 87-floor skyscraper, which also has a viewing platform
(32 London Bridge Street).

66___Morden Hall Park

On the edge of London

Want to trade London's hustle, noise and congestion for the delightful sights and sounds of the open countryside? Simply take the Northern Line to its southern end, Morden, and walk a few minutes. At Morden Hall Park you'll find meandering streams – tributaries to the river River Wandle (see ch. 106) – crossed by picturesque footbridges framing the view of Morden Hall, a handsome, white, 18th century manor house originally built for the Garth family between 1750 and 1765.

In 1873 the wealthy merchant Gilliat Hatfeild bought the hall. He had grown up at Morden Cottage next to the mills powered by the River Wandle. The mills were used to grind dried tobacco leaves, sold as snuff to fashionable 19th century gentlemen. Hatfeild created the park from the surrounding land, built bridges, planted trees such as willow and chestnut, laid out an orchard and erected new buildings. Hatfeild's son turned the hall into a convalescent home from World War I onwards, preferring to live in Morden Cottage. He created a rose garden containing more than 2,000 roses across 38 flowerbeds, and tended it until his death in 1942, when everything was left to the National Trust.

Today's visitors can enjoy tea and coffee at the café in the renovated stable yard, browse the second-hand bookshop and see changing exhibitions in the Living Green Centre. The restored waterwheel highlights the park's industrial past. The 123-acre site also contains a wetlands area at the north end of the park. It features a 200-metre-long boardwalk from which you can watch waterfowl like herons or seasonally visiting egrets, and dip for newts and frogs. With luck you will also spot the native kingfisher: the female bird can be recognised by the pinky-orange tinge to the lower part of her beak. In order to be accepted as a suitor, the male has to bring her a fish as a present. Why not give yourself the gift of a visit to this park?

Address Morden Hall Road, SM4 5JD, www.nationaltrust.org.uk/morden-hall-park | Getting there Tube to Morden (Northern Line) | Hours Daily 9am–6pm; closing times vary, please check website | Tip You might also want to check out nearby Morden Park with its ancient monument and 69-acre nature reserve.

67__Mount Street Gardens

90 benches in a warmer climate

The tall, red-brick mansion blocks and two churches surrounding this Mayfair garden create a warm microclimate that allows for more unusual and exotic plants than elsewhere in London. Imposing London plane trees provide the canopy for a mimosa (*Acacia dealbata*), a Canary Island date palm (*Phoenix canariensis*) and a Chusan palm (*Trachycarpus fortunei*). Three dawn redwoods (*Metasequoia glyptostroboides*) are planted together on the lawn with a corkscrew willow (*Salix matsudana tortuosa*). There are also camellias, hollies and laurels, which thrive in the shady areas under the trees.

Before Mount Street Gardens became a public garden it was the burial ground for the parish church of St George Hanover Square from 1725. Adjacent to the churchyard in the north was the parish workhouse, which became so overcrowded that another site was acquired and it was relocated in 1871. The burial ground was closed in 1854 following an Act of Parliament prohibiting all burials in Central London because of health risks. A later Act enabled 'open spaces and burial grounds in the Metropolis for the use of the inhabitants thereof for exercise and recreation'. The gardens were laid out in 1889–90, more or less to the current design.

A bronze drinking fountain with lion head spouts topped by a rearing horse was designed by Sir Ernest George and Harold Peto in 1891. The sculptures in the gardens include a horse's head – *Fire* by Nic Fiddian-Green – and a giraffe given to the City of Westminster by the Italian Republic. Another striking feature is the over 90 welcoming wooden benches. Many Americans frequent the little park as the US embassy is in nearby Grosvenor Square. Some of them loved the garden so much that they wanted to leave their mark with an inscription on a bench: 'Seymour Augenbraun – a New Yorker and artist for whom this spot in London is his oasis of beauty...'

Address South Audley Street, W1K 2TH, myparks.westminster.gov.uk/parks/
mount-street-gardens | Getting there Tube to Green Park (Victoria, Piccadilly and Jubilee
Lines) | Hours Daily 8am–dusk | Tip Visit the Church of the Immaculate Conception
or Farm Street Church adjacent to the garden with an altar designed by Pugin, who also
designed the interior of the Palace of Westminster.

68_Mudchute Park and Farm
Old MacDonald had a farm…

Just like in the song, you hear neighing, baaing, clucking, quacking and oinking when you approach Mudchute Park and Farm on London's Isle of Dogs. More than 100 animals live here! There are Dexter cattle, Oxford Down sheep, Anglo-Nubian goats, Tamworth and pot-bellied pigs, horses, ponies, donkeys, llamas and alpacas, Dumbo rats, cockatiels, diamond doves, Transylvanian Naked Neck chicken, geese, ducks and many other species. Many of them are rare-breed British farm animals. With 32 acres of land this is not only one of the largest inner-city farms in Europe but also a nature reserve and a charity.

The area got its name when it was used to deposit spoil from the excavation of Millwall Dock in the 1860s. In 1974 there were plans to build a high-rise estate here, but the locals fought successfully against it and formed the Mudchute Association to preserve nature and to create a 'people's park'. They planted trees and introduced farm animals and horses.

An equestrian centre is part of the farm, offering horse-riding lessons at different levels for individuals and groups. Farm tours and animal encounter sessions can be booked. You can also do chicken-keeping or dog-training courses here. Corporate groups as well as locals can volunteer on the farm. The Mudchute Kitchen, the local café, serves delicious breakfasts, brunches and cakes, all made on the premises. In the little shop you can buy wool from Mudchute sheep, bags and badges. Along with the numerous animals the park also contains a range of wildlife habitats including woodlands, wetlands, meadows and field margins. Wildflowers here include cow parsley and bladder campion, dog rose and chicory. The wildflowers attract butterflies like the brimstone and the red admiral and other insects such as bees, grasshoppers and beetles. Old MacDonald's farm probably looked just like this.

Address Pier Street, Isle of Dogs, E14 3HP, www.mudchute.org, farm@mudchute.org | **Getting there** Train to Crossharbour (Dockland Light Railway) | **Hours** Daily dawn–dusk | **Tip** For great views of Canary Wharf walk to neighbouring Millwall Park. In autumn it hosts the London Octoberfest.

69__New River Walk

Fresh water for London

The New River Walk in Islington is hard to find, and locals who know about it jealously guard its secret location. Running parallel to busy Essex Road, it is basically a green corridor running alongside a narrow stretch of water. Part of an old and much larger canal system, it is steeped in the history of London's waterways. Looking deceptively like a river, it consists in fact of two ponds at the London end of the New River, an artificial canal. Sir Hugh Myddleton, a Welsh polymath and jeweller to King James I, was the brain behind the scheme that brought clean water from springs in Herefordshire to the City of London in 1613. Today the actual New River runs in pipes underground.

The five-acre park between St Paul's Road and Canonbury Road was first planted in the 1860s and was re-opened as a public space in 1954. In the summer months the narrow winding path along the water offers enchanting views at each turn. The ambler passes wooden bridges and a little round brick hut, originally built for the linesman, whose job it was to guard the river and prevent fishing and swimming. Mature trees, among them graceful weeping willows, cherries, swamp cypress, dawn redwood and a pair of sweet gum trees, named for their fragrant sap, line the water and their foliage plays with light and shadow on the smooth surface. Rambling wild roses, corkscrew hazels, Chinese dogwood, fragrant mock orange bushes, flag irises and grasses contribute to the idyllic picture. The still waters are also a haven for coots, moorhens, ducks and even an occasional heron. Terrapins and turtles are less welcome visitors here as they prey on the local wildlife.

Beyond Canonbury Road, 'Astey's Row Rock Garden, Islington's cheddar gorge', strewn with large rocks, continues the green corridor. It's a short relaxing walk and there are plenty of benches – and 'watering holes' – on the way!

Address St Paul's Road/Canonbury Grove, Canonbury Villas & Astey's Row, N1 2PU, www.londongardenstrust.org/features/NewRiver.htm | **Getting there** Tube to Highbury & Islington (Victoria Line) or London Overground to Canonbury (North London and East London Lines) | **Hours** Daily 8am–dusk | **Tip** Visit the 'talking' statue of Sir Hugh Myddleton on Islington Green and talk to him on the phone!

70__Osterley Park and House

A country estate in London

Surrounded by 331 acres of gardens, park and farmland, Osterley Park and House, once a Tudor country estate, is now part of urban Hounslow. Sir Thomas Gresham commissioned the original manor in 1576 but Osterley's biggest transformation came about through the Child family, wealthy bankers who bought the estate in 1711. In 1761 Sir Francis Child commissioned Robert Adam to redevelop Osterley House in the neoclassical style, and after his death his brother Robert continued to employ Adam for the interiors.

Today's visitors travel back to the 1780s. Roman statues line the walls of the entrance hall and Greek pottery motifs adorn the walls of the 'Etruscan' dressing room. Not only the house is neoclassical; Adam also left his mark on the gardens where he created the Garden House, now sheltering a collection of lemon trees. The park was most likely re-designed by Mrs Robert Child and her steward Mr Bunce. She could see the garden from her dressing room and personally ordered the most fashionable new plants. She also had a menagerie with a collection of exotic birds.

The long walk affords beautiful views of Osterley House and allowed the Child family to show off their handsome brick manor to visitors, who also enjoyed pleasure boating on the Garden Lake. A six-year restoration project has returned many of the structures and features of the 18th century garden. One of them is the recreation of Mrs Child's flower garden with insular flowerbeds blooming all summer. The Childs even planted an American Border, where they showcased North American trees, shrubs and flowers. The recently created Winter Garden stands out with colourful barks and berries when other parts of the garden lie dormant.

Even now that London has grown around Osterley, it has preserved the calm and serene atmosphere of a true country estate, complete with grazing Charolais cattle.

Address Jersey Road, Isleworth, Middlesex, TW7 4RB, www.nationaltrust.org.uk/ osterley-park-and-house | **Getting there** Tube to Osterley (Piccadilly Line) | **Hours** Daily 10am–5pm in summer, 10am–dusk in winter | **Tip** Take a whole day off and visit nearby Syon Park with equally beautiful gardens (www.syonpark.co.uk).

71 Parkland Walk

Spriggan in the Northern Heights

London's longest and maybe most unusual nature reserve is nearly two-and-a-half miles long but only a few meters wide. Parkland Walk, also known as Northern Heights in North London, began its life as railway tracks that ran between Finsbury Park and Alexandra Park in the late 19th century. The line closed in 1957 and the tracks were lifted in 1972. Platforms and buildings were demolished and Parkland Walk opened in 1984. Connecting three major North London parks, it became an important wildlife corridor. Over 200 species of wild flowers grow here, and although there are few veteran trees because the embankment used to be mowed, the variety of trees and shrubs is astonishing, among them birch, cherry, apple, ash, hazel, elder, hawthorne and English oak.

A special habitat is the patch of acid grassland in the Islington section (between Mountview Road overbridge and Blythwood Road entrance gate), which supports specialised plants and animals such as the cuckoo bee (*Nomada lathburiana*) and its host the mining bee *(Andrena cineraria)*.

Early-morning visitors will hear a remarkable dawn chorus in spring. Next to the more common species, rare birds like the grey wagtail are also sometimes spotted. About 23 species of butterflies live here too, as do several bats such as pipistrelle, Daubenton's and brown long-eared bats. There's even a bat cave in a disused tunnel near Highgate Station. Other mammals include foxes, hedgehogs and rarely seen muntjac deer. But even rarer than that is the Spriggan, a mythical creature from Cornish fairy lore. Spriggans are small thieves, guarding buried treasure, but they can swell to enormous size. If you look up at the arches near the old Crouch End station you'll see the Spriggan grinning down at you. The sculpture was created by Marilyn Collins in the 1990s and inspired Stephen King to write the short horror story, *Crouch End*.

Address Archway Road, N4 3EY, www.parkland-walk.org.uk | Getting there Tube to Highgate (Northern Line) | Hours Unrestricted | Tip Pay attention to the interesting graffiti on the walk!

72 __ Postman's Park

A unique memorial

It's always lovely to encounter a green space in the centre of London, even if it is not very big. Postman's Park, near St Paul's Cathedral and the Museum of London, was created from several churchyards. It's called Postman's Park because the General Post Office used to be nearby and the workers had their lunchtime here. There are some nice mature trees, an impressive banana plant, a lovely fountain and colourful flowerbeds – but this isn't why people come here and stay for hours!

Something else makes this small park truly unique: the Watts Memorial, built by the symbolist painter George Frederic Watts in 1900. In order to commemorate the Golden Jubilee of Queen Victoria, Watts suggested the installation of a 'Memorial to Heroic Self Sacrifice', remembering people who died saving others. Despite his scheme being rejected, Watts carried on and finally realised the memorial in the form of a covered gallery with commemorative glazed Doulton tiles running along its back wall. Before he died, Watts added 13 plaques to the wall, and his wife Mary commissioned another 34.

Nowadays you often see people standing in front of the wall for a long time, studying the deeply moving inscriptions. One of them says: 'Sarah Smith, pantomime artiste at Prince's Theatre died of terrible injuries received when attempting in her inflammable dress to extinguish the flames which had enveloped her companion. January 24 1863.' Another one reads: 'Henry James Bristow aged eight – at Walthamstow on December 30 1890 – saved his little sister's life by tearing off her flaming clothes but caught fire himself and died of burns and shock.' There was a seventy-year gap during which no tiles were added but in 2009 another tablet was unveiled paying tribute to Leigh Pitt who selflessly rescued a child from drowning. A newly revived tradition, hopefully to be continued.

Address St Martin's Le Grand, EC1A 4EU, www.postmanspark.org.uk | **Getting there** Tube to St Paul's (Central Line) or Barbican (Circle, Hammersmith & City and Metropolitan Lines) | **Hours** Daily 8am–7.30pm | **Tip** The Museum of London is just around the corner (150 London Wall) or visit Barts Pathology Museum (3rd Floor, Robin Brook Centre, West Smithfield) with interesting specimens on display!

73 Primrose Hill

Mother Shipton, murder and… Martians?

This North London height is well known for its almost 360-degree views over London. It has also been at the centre of a gloomy prediction and a murder mystery, and nearly became a cemetery. Still it has managed to inspire, as it did William Blake, whose words are inscribed on the summit's York stone edging: 'I have conversed with the spiritual sun. I saw him on Primrose Hill.'

The summit was a place of Druid worship and has been treeless since the Middle Ages. It inspired the medieval soothsayer Ursula Southeil, aka Mother Shipton, to say: 'When London surrounds Primrose Hill, the streets of the metropolis will run with blood.' Not quite, but a mysterious murder did occur in 1678 during the anti-Catholic movement when Sir Edmund Berry Godfrey, a stout supporter of Protestantism, was discovered impaled on his own sword in a ditch at the bottom of the hill. His murderer was never found but several Catholics were executed for plotting to kill him.

At the beginning of the 19th century Primrose Hill was in the running to become one of London's much needed new cemeteries but the owners of the land, Eton College and Lord Southampton, swopped it for land owned by the Crown. Following local pressure, the 62-acre park opened to the public in 1842.

Today's space is mainly open parkland intersected by footpaths with benches and cast-iron streetlights. Among the mature trees on the slopes are hawthorn, horse chestnut, whitebeam and oak. There are a few flowerbeds, a children's playground and a drinking fountain, installed by the Bands of Hope charity.

This magical place will likely survive an alien invasion such as H G Wells described in his novel *The War of the Worlds*, where the aliens make their final base on Primrose Hill. Tourists walk up here to enjoy the view, and at night teenagers gather on the summit to… do whatever teenagers do, but aliens have yet to be sighted.

Address Primrose Hill Road, NW3 3AX, www.royalparks.org.uk | Getting there Tube to Chalk Farm (Northern Line) | Tip For refreshments after your walk check out Regent's Park Road toward Chalk Farm Station, which offers a choice of cafés and restaurants.

74 __ Queen Elizabeth Olympic Park

On your marks, get set, go!

This park is well known for its great sporting venues and for the event that brought them to life: the London 2012 Olympics.

When the Olympic fire was extinguished on 12 August, 2012 it didn't signify the end of the park but a new beginning for a previously underdeveloped urban area, earning it the catchy moniker, 'Olympicopolis'. The park not only provides countless sporting opportunities; the exploration of nature and art play an equally important role in this sustainably managed green space.

With 560 acres of parkland, it's the biggest urban park created in the UK for over a century, and is unashamedly modern. It is based on the concept of 'Green Infrastructure': a network of green spaces building with nature that becomes an integrated part of its environment. Hundreds of new habitats were created and more than 6,000 trees planted, among them London plane, oak, birch, crab apple, hawthorn, alder, aspen, mountain ash and elm, as well as rare species such as the declining native black poplar.

Dedicated gardens invite the visitor to explore. One of them, The Great British Garden, co-designed by 11-year-old Hannah Clegg, offers not only lovely planted borders and fruiting hedges but also a frog pond where dipping is encouraged. The famous garden designer Piet Oudolf created his trademark prairie style in the Pleasure Gardens.

The park is liberally dotted with public art works, the biggest of which is the *ArcelorMittal Orbit*, Britain's largest public sculpture, which doubles as an observation tower. Combining sculpture and structural engineering, it was created by artist Sir Anish Kapoor and engineer Cecil Balmond. Since 2016 it also features the world's longest slide (178 metres). Why don't you give it a try? On your marks, get set, go!

Address Westfield Avenue, E20 2ST, www.queenelizabetholympicpark.co.uk, customerservices@queenelizabetholympicpark.co.uk | **Getting there** Tube (Central and Jubilee Lines), London Overground (North London Line) or Docklands Light Railway to Stratford | **Hours** Unrestricted | **Tip** Use one of the four trails (London 2012, children's, art, and parkland and wildlife) to explore the park.

75__Queen's Park
Walking in circles

You can actually do that in Queen's Park because its paths wind into a figure of eight, designed by Alexander McKenzie (who also created Alexandra Palace Park). In 1879 part of the land was used for the Royal Kilburn Agricultural Show, showcasing agricultural machinery, a working dairy and a range of farm animals. The City of London Corporation purchased the site in 1886. A legacy by William Ward 'to be applied and expended in the erection of some institution… for the benefit of the poorer classes' made it possible to proceed with the installation of a splash of green for the community. The park was originally named Kilburn Recreation Ground but as it was opened in 1887, the year of Queen Victoria's Golden Jubilee, permission was granted to name the park after the queen.

McKenzie designed the park in a natural style with curves rather than straight lines, without any architectural features, only trees, shrubs and open areas of lawn for sports. The relaxed design and informal feeling of the garden was opposed by the architectural press of the time as they favoured the more formal style Joseph Paxton had applied at Crystal Palace Park. McKenzie's design turned out to be forward-looking because today, while preserving its original layout, the 30-acre park offers everything needed in a modern community park. It has tennis courts, a pitch and putt course, a petanque pitch as well as a 19th century bandstand. Children love the playground with its big sandpit and paddling pool. Another children's favourite is the Pet Corner with chickens, rabbits and goats. The woodland walk was created in the 1990s and there is grassland with wildflowers and hedgerows. The best spot for bookworms is the Quiet Garden near the mock-Tudor shelter in the southeast corner of the park. It was laid out in 1966 with ornamental flower beds and lots of benches. Here you can sit and read on a bench dedicated to Rosemary Hinkley, 'who loved to read here'.

Address Harvist Road, NW6 6SG, www.cityoflondon.gov.uk/things-to-do/green-spaces | **Getting there** Tube (Bakerloo Line) or London Overground (Watford DC Line) to Queen's Park | **Hours** Daily 7am–dusk | **Tip** Visit Paddington Old Cemetery just across Salusbury Road with its beautiful chapels and beehives that produce 'tombstone honey'. It was also the location for an episode of *Doctor Who*.

76 Queen Square Gardens
Hospitals, queens and Sam the cat

The dominating feature in this garden is the lead statue of a queen looking down sternly on a bed of roses. There has been some confusion over her identity. Is she Queen Anne, Queen Mary or Queen Caroline? And which queen was the square named after? A consensus was reached and the statue is now thought to depict Queen Charlotte, wife of King George III. She has cause to look worried as the king was actually treated in a house in Queen Square for his mental illness. It is said that she rented a cellar in one of the houses to store food for the king during his treatment. The house is now a pub called The Queen's Larder.

The square, originally called Devonshire Square, was laid out in 1716–1725 and probably renamed after the reigning Queen Anne. Famous residents were the writer Fanny Burney (1752–1840) and William Morris, who moved his company here in 1865.

In the 19th century the aristocratic and artistic residents were replaced with medical institutions. Today the park is surrounded by hospitals: the National Hospital for Neurology and Neurosurgery, the London Hospital for Integrated Medicine and the former Italian Hospital for poor Italian emigrants, founded by the Italian businessman Giovanni Battista Ortelli in 1884. It is now part of Great Ormond Street Hospital, also nearby. Often you'll see patients and visitors sitting on benches enjoying a few rays of sunshine. Some of the benches commemorate the 16 doctors who died in the Tristar air disaster of 1972.

Statues here include a bronze torso of a mother holding a child, by the sculptor Patricia Finch. It was acquired by the Friends of the Children of Great Ormond Street Hospital in memory of Andrew Meller. And then there is 'Sam the cat' reaching down from a brick column. He is dedicated to Penny (Patricia Penn 1914–1992), a champion of local causes – and cat lover.

Address Queen Square, WC1N 3AT | Getting there Tube to Russell Square (Piccadilly Line) | Hours Daily 7.30am–dusk | Tip At Cagney's you can get reasonably priced great American food (13 Cosmo Place).

77 Red Cross Garden

An open-air sitting room

'Walks wind about between small lawns and flower-beds set with flowering trees and shrubs. Two plane trees are planted on the larger spaces of gravel, which are to have circular seats round them, and where we hope working women will sit and rest and do needlework, and tired men sit and smoke on summer evenings.' This is how Octavia Hill, the social reformer who founded this garden, envisioned it in a letter she wrote in 1887. Also a founder of the National Trust, Hill thought it was essential for workers to have access to nature and supported the development of new public open spaces. She conceived the social housing scheme with two rows of cottages and a community hall, designed by Elijah Hoole, to which the garden belongs. It was laid out by Emmeline Sieveking and Fanny Wilkinson with curved lawns, an ornamental pond with fountain, a bandstand and a play area. After its opening in 1888, the garden quickly became a social hub hosting the Southwark Flower Show and other events.

After years of neglect, when it became a flat space with areas of grass and tarmac, the restoration of the garden overseen by the Red Cross Garden Group took place in 2005. Many of the original Victorian features were restored, among them a mosaic depicting a sower, donated by Julia Minet.

The garden is now maintained by the Bankside Open Spaces Trust and received a prestigious Green Flag Award in 2016. There is a pond covered with water lilies that sports a little fountain, a rock garden, meandering paths, a small bridge and numerous benches. The English-cottage-garden-style planting includes foxgloves, hollyhocks and scented roses. Today it is again a joy to sit here on a summer evening even if you forget your needlework and don't smoke. One of the neighbouring cats might visit you on your bench; The Shard visible in the background adds a modern touch to the open-air sitting room.

Address 50 Redcross Way, SE1 1HA, www.bost.org.uk/open-places/red-cross-garden, info@bost.org.ok | **Getting there** Tube to Borough (Northern Line) | **Hours** Daily dawn–dusk | **Tip** Nearby Crossbones Garden is a former pauper graveyard where the 'outcast dead' are remembered.

78__Regent's Canal
When is a garden not a garden?

This is not exactly a park, nor is it a garden, but it received a Green Flag Award in 2015/2016. It runs through several major London parks and is over eight miles long. The Regent's Canal and towpath is the most relaxed way to explore London sights and you have a choice of walking, cycling or taking a boat.

The canal leads from Little Venice to Limehouse Basin and connects the Grand Union Canal system to the Thames. It was completed in 1820 by the Regent's Canal Company in association with John Nash, who designed Regent's Park at the time.

There's so much to see along the way that it's best to walk or cycle the towpath in stages, and maybe take the waterbus from Little Venice to Camden Lock. Between Little Venice and Regent's Park you'll pass Lisson Grove Moorings and its colourful narrow boats and tiny but beautiful gardens. The boat stops at London Zoo and you can purchase tickets on the waterbus to avoid the queues. Nearby in the Cumberland Basin lies the Feng Shang Princess, a bright red, two-storey Chinese restaurant on a houseboat.

There are quite a few unusual barges along the way. In Little Venice you'll find a floating puppet theatre and at Granary Square near King's Cross a book barge called Word On The Water is moored. A bit further to the east it's worth stopping at the London Canal Museum, where you can learn everything about the history of London's canals, the boats and the horses that pulled them, as well as see the huge Victorian ice well in the basement where ice from Norway was stored. On your way to Limehouse you'll pass Victoria Park and Mile End Park. Take another break at the Ragged School Museum, which offers lessons in a Victorian school. After 800 more metres you'll arrive at Limehouse Basin. Don't forget to look out for the ramps that were used to pull the horses out that had fallen into the canal!

Address Starting point Warwick Avenue, W9 2PT, www.canalrivertrust.org.uk/
enjoy-the-waterways/canal-and-river-network/regents-canal | Getting there Tube to
Warwick Avenue (Bakerloo Line) for Little Venice or train to Limehouse (c2c) for
Limehouse Basin | Hours Unrestricted | Tip In Little Venice take a little detour to
Paddington Basin and admire the unusual bridges here, including the Fan Bridge, the
Rolling Bridge and the Helix Bridge.

79 __ Regent's Park
'Rose is a rose'

This phrase from Gertrude Stein's poem 'Sacred Emily' certainly comes to mind when visiting Queen Mary's Garden in The Regent's Park. At its best in the first two weeks in June, the garden located in the Inner Circle of the 395-acre park contains an abundance of more than 12,000 roses of 400 varieties, ranging from climbers and ramblers to floribundas and hybrid teas. You'll see people walking around sniffing the gloriously scented English roses or repeating their names under their breath to remember them for their own gardens.

The rose garden is not the only floral extravaganza in this exceedingly formal and elaborate park. As many of the Royal Parks did, it started out as royal hunting grounds. Commissioned by the future King George IV and designed by the architect John Nash, the park opened to the public in 1835. One of the features planned by Nash, The Avenue Gardens, did not thrive and was re-designed by the Victorian garden designer William Andrews Nesfield. In the centre of these formal gardens with a wealth of Victorian-style bedding plants and tiered fountains stands the 'Lion Vase, a stone bowl supported by four winged lions.

A secret favourite of many visitors are the more secluded and less showy gardens of St John's Lodge to the north of the Inner Circle. Completed in 1819 the lodge is now privately owned by the royal family of Brunei; the garden has been open to the public since 1928. It consists of a series of compartments with sculptures, designed by Robert Weir Schultz in 1889 for the Marquess of Bute who wanted a 'garden fit for meditation'.

Yet, there is more to admire: The Japanese Garden, which is actually an island complete with waterfall and bridge, the Delphinium Border and the Mediterranean Borders – and these are only the horticultural delights. Don't forget the London Zoo, which alone takes a day to visit.

Address Chester Road, NW1 4NR, www.royalparks.org.uk/parks/the-regents-park |
Getting there Tube to Regent's Park (Bakerloo Line) | Hours Daily 5am–dusk | Tip
If you want to do something quintessentially English attend a cricket game at Lord's,
walking distance to the west of the park (www.lords.org).

80_ Richmond Park

Here's to the oak

The most impressive features of a park are its ancient trees, and in Richmond Park, at 2,350 acres the largest of the Royal Parks, there are 1,200 of them, most of them oaks. Each single oak tree supports hundreds of species, among them a diversity of fungi, bats, birds and beetles. Some endangered beetles, which depend on decaying wood, can be found here, including the rusty click beetle, the cardinal click beetle and the stag beetle. Other wildlife include foxes, rabbits, shrews, mice, voles and nine species of bats. You are also likely to come across the 630-strong population of red and fallow deer, roaming freely in the park since 1637. The park is also home to around 144 different bird species ranging from owls and kestrels to skylarks and waterfowl.

Richmond Park's long history as a hunting park began in the 14th century. It became a Royal deer park under Henry VII and was enclosed by Charles I. The landscape consists of woodland, open grassland and several ponds, which were mainly created by gravel digging in the late 17th century.

Inside the park are two historic manor houses: Pembroke Lodge, altered by Sir John Soane and today an event venue with tea rooms; and White Lodge, home to the Royal Ballet School. From King Henry's Mound in Pembroke Lodge Gardens you have panoramic views over the Thames Valley to the west and St Paul's Cathedral to the east. Henry VIII supposedly stood here to watch a rocket fired from the Tower of London, the sign that Anne Boleyn had been executed for treason.

Another important part of the park is Isabella Plantation, a 40-acre woodland garden with a large collection of camellias, rhododendrons and azaleas, which line the ponds and streams and flower fully in May and June. But don't miss winter here, when ancient oaks are especially beautiful with the low light highlighting their grained wood.

Address Holly Lodge, Richmond, TW10 5HS, www.royalparks.org.uk/parks/richmond-park |
Getting there Tube to Richmond (District Line), then bus 371 or 65 to Richmond Park |
Hours Unrestricted for pedestrians, except Nov and Feb: 7.30am–8pm | Tip Visit also
nearby Ham House, one of the grandest Stuart houses in Britain (www.nationaltrust.org.uk/
ham-house-and-garden).

81 Royal Botanic Gardens Kew

148,008 plants and a compost heap

This number is your clue to what Kew Gardens is all about. It's a research institution with laboratories, gardens, plant collections, a library, the Millennium Seed Bank and 700 staff, all aiming to understand plants and fungi, which form the basis of life on earth.

But it is also a very attractive garden with close to two million visitors per year and an incredible number of plant species (13,808) that not only have useful properties but often also flower beautifully.

Each of the glasshouses transports you to a different world. They include the Waterlily House filled with giant Victoria amazonica; the Palm House with its rainforest climate and collection of palms and other tropical species; the Princess of Wales Conservatory, containing ten different climactic environments ranging from dry tropics to wet tropics and environments for ferns, orchids and carnivorous plants; and the Alpine House with the cool, dry conditions the plants prefer.

The 300 acres also embrace further, distinctive gardens, such as the arboretum with 14,000 trees, some of them dating back to when the garden first opened to visitors in 1841. It was already a botanic garden in the 18th century and parts of it, such as Kew Palace, were a royal residence of George II and Queen Caroline. Today only plants grown in the 17th century and before are planted in the Queen's Garden. Other historic structures include the Pagoda, completed in 1762, and Queen Charlotte's Cottage, her private retreat.

There are many more wonderful things to explore, such as the vertiginous Treetop Walkway, Kid's Kew and The Hive. Also, the 320-metre-long Great Broad Walk Borders were refurbished and re-opened in 2016 and form the longest double herbaceous border in the country. But none of the plants here could exist without one of the largest compost heaps in Europe.

Address Richmond, Surrey TW9 3AE, www.kew.org | Getting there Tube (District Line) or London Overground (North London Line) to Kew Gardens | Hours Mon–Thu 10am–6.30pm; Fri–Sun and bank holidays 10am–7.30pm | Tip The Victorian Kew Gardens Station is Grade II listed and is the only London tube station with its own pub.

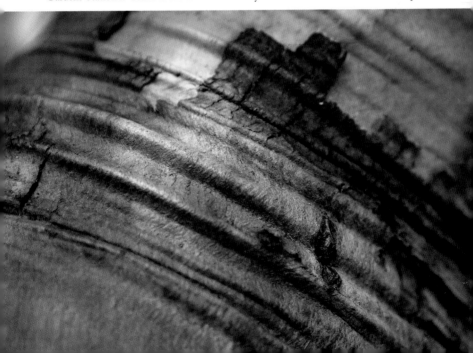

82__Shepherdess Walk Park

A pleasure garden

At first glance there's not much to look at in Shepherdess Walk Park in Hackney. It is a small neighbourhood park with trees, lawns and a children's play area, but tucked away in a corner of this green space is something very special: a Roman mosaic – by the looks of it – covering two perpendicular walls and parts of the pavement! But don't be fooled by the flowing clothes of the people depicted. If you step closer you'll realise that these murals don't depict Roman gods and goddesses but scenes of everyday life in Hackney's parks and open spaces. One of them is called *History In The Making* and another, *Hackney 2012*. They depict scenes in Hackney Parks throughout the year, so you see joggers and skateboarders, people playing Frisbee, having a picnic or going for a swim. Others are listening to their iPods, working with a leaf blower, walking dogs or flying kites. Two protruding panels are dedicated to the makers and funders of the mosaic. The mural on the far wall, *Shepherdess Walk*, features two shepherdesses, sheep, birds and hares. Each sheep's coat has a different pattern, and a beautiful floral border frames the picture. The pavement mosaics depict wildflowers and insects that flourish in inner-city areas.

The wall mosaics were designed by the artist Tessa Hunkin and made by volunteers from Lifeline (a group that helps people with addiction problems) and other local communities. Tessa's work is inspired by Roman and early Christian mosaics but these murals couldn't be more local. They relate to the history of the park, which in the 18th century was the pleasure garden of a pub called The Shepherd and Shepherdess, where cakes and cream were served, and which was later renamed The Eagle.

The project, funded by Hackney Borough, was also created to capture the spirit of the 2012 Olympic Games. It has definitely captured the spirit of life in Hackney: a real pleasure garden!

Address Shepherdess Walk, N1 7JN, www.hackney.gov.uk/shepherdess-walk | **Getting there** Tube to Angel (Northern Line) | **Hours** Unrestricted | **Tip** If you are a popcorn fan check out Propercorn, which sells many different types of sweet and salty popcorn (41 Wenlock Road).

83__Skip Garden
More rhubarb, less rubble

The King's Cross area is believed to be the location of the legendary battle between Queen Boudicca and the Roman invaders. The queen herself is allegedly buried between platform nine and ten at King's Cross Station, a fact well known to J K Rowling when she created the legendary platform for the Hogwarts Express. The name 'King's Cross' has its origin in a statue of King George IV, which stood in the area from 1830 to 1845 – when it was demolished because it was so unpopular.

The area around the two major stations has been redeveloped in the last decades. Major art and science institutions such as Central Saint Martins and the Crick Institute moved here and attracted further development. Part of the 67-acre development area is still a building site – and one small garden profits from it. The Skip Garden is the epitome of an urban garden with vegetables and trees growing in skips and in planters made from scaffold boards. Tomatoes, ginger and chillies are cultivated under polytunnels made with water pipes. Recycling building materials from the surrounding construction site is not only sustainable but also saves money. The garden is also a community garden managed by Global Generation, a charity supporting communities working with nature, giving mainly young people the opportunity to learn new skills such as tending beehives, making furniture, creating jams and selling their produce.

The garden is both functional and charming with wildflowers, beehives and chicken coops. The on-site café, Skip Garden Kitchen, serves teas, coffees, cakes and seasonal lunches. There is a cosy Mongolian yurt for shelter and in the evenings fires are lit around the whole garden. The space can be hired for meetings and parties. And the garden has another advantage: it's mobile. Whenever the building starts, it can move to a different site to create more rhubarb and less rubble.

Address Tapper Walk, N1C 4AQ, www.globalgeneration.org.uk, generate@globalgeneration.org.uk | Getting there Tube to King's Cross St Pancras (Circle, Metropolitan, Piccadilly, Hammersmith & City, Northern and Victoria Lines) | Hours Tue–Sat 10am–4pm | Tip Look out for the mysterious lighthouse opposite King's Cross St Pancras Station Square. Was it once advertising an oyster bar? Nobody knows!

84_SOAS Roof Garden
Texture and contemplation

This small, Japanese-inspired roof garden on top of the Brunei Gallery in Bloomsbury is part of The School of Oriental and African Studies (SOAS). It was established during the Japan 2001 celebrations and sponsored by Mr Haruhisa Handa (Toshu Fukami), an Honorary Fellow of the School.

The minimalist garden's designer, Peter Swift, had previously applied Japanese garden design principles to the British climate, and put his experience to good use here. The elements of Japanese gardens mimic nature: raked gravel imitates water; rocks represent islands. The enclosed space is structured by a central rectangular area covered by light grey gravel interspersed with dark grey islands of larvikite stone from Norway. There are also rectangular slabs of basaltic rock that represent bridges over flowing water. This garden is not so much about plants as about different textures of stone. Rectangular sandstone is contrasted with irregular green slate, granite chippings and basaltic rock. Straight lines contrast with curves; light stones are juxtaposed with dark rocks. Plants play a supporting role, sometimes emphasizing and sometimes softening the hard surfaces of the stones, such as the lemon thyme arranged in a chequerboard pattern alternating with gravel. A wisteria covers the pergola and provides flowers in spring and welcome shade in summer.

The garden is dedicated to forgiveness, represented by the kanji character engraved in the small water basin. In bad weather, chain drains rather than downpipes are used to direct rainwater, which turns them into water features. A little platform is open for displays and events ranging from ceramic exhibitions to musical performances. To appreciate the space you should really sit here for a while and look at the different textures. Observe the change of light on the stone surfaces. Maybe a leaf has fallen on the grey slate?

Address Thornhaugh Street, WC1H 0XG, www.soas.ac.uk/soas-life/roofgarden, gallery@soas.ac.uk | **Getting there** Tube to Russell Square (Piccadilly Line) | **Hours** Tue–Sat 10.30am–5pm | **Tip** The Brunei Gallery showcases contemporary and historical exhibitions from Africa, Asia and the Middle East (www.soas.ac.uk/gallery).

85__Southwood Garden
Bells of St James

Just a few steps away from Piccadilly Circus this little garden in the churchyard of St James's Church Piccadilly offers respite and calm for office workers, shoppers and all who need to look at a bit of green and take a breath in London's busy West End. Adding to the charm of the space are the two small markets that take place in front of St James on most days of the week (a food market on Mondays and Tuesdays, an arts and crafts market from Wednesday to Saturday).

For 200 years this spot was used as a burial ground. St James, originally built by Christopher Wren in 1684, suffered severe bomb damage during World War II and the Labour politician Viscount Southwood donated money to convert the churchyard into a garden of remembrance dedicated to the people of London for their fortitude and sacrifice during the war. Queen Mary opened the garden in 1946. A fountain by Alfred F Hardiman with bronze cherubs riding dolphins commemorates Southwood. Another sculpture by Hardiman depicts a female figure called Peace. The garden also contains a statue of St Mary of Nazareth by Sir Charles Wheeler and a canopied external pulpit.

The garden was refurbished and replanted for the 2012 Olympics, creating biodiverse habitats in a small green space surrounded by stone and concrete. Contributing to the upkeep is the coffee chain Costa, which also sends two of their workers every month to help the gardener employed by the church. Under the ubiquitous London planes, the planting includes a mulberry tree, a yew tree and several shadbushes (*Amelanchier*). There are shade-loving perennials like hostas and plenty of flowering bulbs in spring. The planting is designed in waves, echoing the rhythm of life at St James.

In the background of it all, during the busy times as well as the quieter ones, you'll hear the bells of St James ringing out on the half hour.

Address 197 Piccadilly, W1J 9LL, www.sjp.org.uk | Getting there Tube to Piccadilly Circus (Bakerloo and Piccadilly Lines) | Hours Unrestricted | Tip If you are interested in beautiful and rare antiquarian books and prints, visit Henry Sotheran (2–5 Sackville Street).

86 Spa Fields Park
Radical history in Islington

Close to lively Exmouth Market, dogs and their owners gather in this park for a chat in the morning and children populate the playground and lawns in the afternoon. There is an outdoor gym, tennis courts, a lavender garden, borders planted with scented roses, and several gnarled trees. It's a green and peaceful neighbourhood outlet used and enjoyed by many residents.

But it was not always like this. When the plot was still mainly open ground with springs and ponds, the London Spaw pub opened here in 1685 and gave the area its name. In the 18th century the working classes came here seeking diversion. A domed entertainment venue called the Pantheon was popular for tea parties, drinking and socialising, but only a few years after opening in 1770 the building was turned into a Dissenting chapel by the pious Countess of Huntingdon.

In 1816 Spa Fields nearly became the site of a British revolution. Ten thousand people gathered to support a petition demanding universal (male) suffrage, annual general elections and secret ballot. Henry 'Orator' Hunt tried to present the petition to the Prince Regent but the prince refused to see him. A second gathering at Spa Fields with over 20,000 people turned violent; a pedestrian was killed and the rioters were arrested.

But there is an even darker chapter in the history of the park. In the 1780s the garden of the Pantheon had been turned into a burial ground with space for 2,700 burials. As it was cheaper being buried here than in local churchyards, the grounds soon became overcrowded and over a period of 50 years, 80,000 internments took place. Body snatchers were given free reign, bodies were exhumed and burned to make room for fresh burials. These practices were revealed in 1845, and led to the closure of the cemetery. Spa Fields became a public park in 1886 and has been a place of recreation and entertainment ever since.

Address Skinner Street, EC1R, www.islington.gov.uk | Getting there Train to Farringdon (Thameslink) | Hours Unrestricted | Tip It is worth visiting The Charterhouse, a former Carthusian monastery turned almshouse in a beautiful 14th century building, which opened as a museum in January 2017 (www.thecharterhouse.org).

87 __ St Dunstan in the East

Destined to be a garden

The small green space amongst the ruins of a Gothic church half-way between London Bridge and Tower Bridge is one of the most romantic gardens in Central London. There are several garden rooms to wander in, each one equipped with benches. The walls are covered in climbers and the arched Gothic windows allow tantalising glimpses of other little garden rooms. The planting also includes seasonal flower beds, palm trees and more unusual specimens such as a winter's bark tree (*Drimys winteri)* whose bark was used to prevent scurvy, and a stumpy fig tree, planted to commemorate the crowning of King George VI in 1937.

During its long history the church was damaged and rebuilt several times. The first church on the site was built in 1100, with the south aisle added in 1391. This aisle had to be repaired in the 17th century and only 35 years later, in 1666, the whole building was severely damaged in the Great Fire of London. It was patched up during the following years and Sir Christopher Wren added a tower and a spire between 1695 and 1701. He built it in the Gothic style to match the old church. In the early 19th century the church fell again into disrepair and was rebuilt in 1817–21 by David Laing. Disaster struck once more during the Blitz in 1941 and this time not much survived, except for Wren's steeple and tower. It was decided not to rebuild the church but the spire was reconstructed in 1953 and the tower was refurbished in 1970-71.

The garden was created by the City of London in 1971. St Dunstan's career as a church ended with the decision not to rebuild it but now it lives a new life as one of London's favourite secret gardens. One is tempted to suspect that the church was destined to become a garden. The best time to come here is at the weekend, when all the office workers have gone home and the little garden is very quiet and nearly becomes a church again.

Address St Dunstan's Hill, EC3R 5DD, www.cityoflondon.gov.uk | Getting there Tube to Monument or Tower Hill (Circle and District Lines) | Hours Daily 8am–7pm or dusk, whichever is earlier | Tip Visit nearby St Mary-At-Hill (EC3R 8EE), another very old church, which was beautifully rebuilt after the Great Fire by Robert Hooke.

88 St George's Gardens

Body snatchers and a muse from a pub

Located today in the Central London area of Bloomsbury, this site was still meadowland at the beginning of the 18th century. It was acquired in 1713 as the burial grounds for the new churches of St George, Bloomsbury Way and St George the Martyr, Queen Square. As such they were the first Anglican burial grounds away from the churches they served. Although a high wall was built around the cemetery, the uptake was slow because grieving relatives feared body snatchers who supplied a nearby anatomy school. This only changed when Robert Nelson, a philanthropist and commissioner of 50 churches, decided to be buried here. But these fears were not unfounded: In 1777 a gravedigger and his assistant were stopped carrying a sack, which proved to contain the body of a Mrs Jane Sainsbury. They became the first people indicted for the theft of a dead body.

The burial grounds were closed in 1854 and turned into public gardens in 1889 following an initiative by the sisters Octavia and Miranda Hill through the Kyrle Society, which promoted the creation of public gardens with the slogan 'Bring Beauty Home to the Poor'. Fanny Wilkinson designed the gardens leaving several of the monuments intact. The most noteworthy include the tomb of Anna Gibson, who died in 1726 and was a granddaughter of Oliver Cromwell, as well as an obelisk built for the jurist and explorer Thomas Falconer in 1729. There are some old trees in the gardens, among them weeping ash, oak, lime and London plane. A line of broken gravestones marks the division between the two burial grounds.

The gardens have a very active friends group that holds annual St George's Day parties here and created a sensory garden in 2008. The terracotta statue of Euterpe, the muse of instrumental music, originally decorated a pub on Tottenham Court Road. She only came here in 1961 but looks as if she has always been here.

Address 62 Marchmont Street, WC1N 1AB, www.friendsofstgeorgesgardens.org.uk |
Getting there Tube to Russell Square (Piccadilly Line) | Hours Daily dawn–dusk | Tip
Those who want to know the difference between a dodo and a quagga will enjoy a visit to
the Grant Museum of Zoology (21 University Street).

89 __ St James's Park

Where are the pelicans?

The famous pelicans in St James's Park are descendants of the first flock given to King Charles II by the Russian ambassador in 1664. That wasn't the end of the pelican-giving tradition, however. As recently as 2013, three birds were given to the park by Prague Zoo. Most of the time they do their best to entertain visitors. One of the birds even used to sit on a bench next to them but sometimes they can be elusive and you can wander through the park without a sighting.

The biggest park feature is the lake, which reaches from Horse Guards Road at one end almost to Buckingham Palace at the other. Water has played an interesting role in the park's history.

Before it became a Royal Park (the oldest in London) it was swampy marshland with a women's leper hospital named James the Less, which gave the park its name. When Henry VIII acquired the land around 1530, he put a fence around it to create one of his many deer parks. He also built a hunting lodge that was later turned into St James's Palace. James I drained the park and created a large pond, channels and islands. He also kept crocodiles, camels and an elephant here. Over the next centuries the park was re-landscaped several times, with the last major changes being implemented in 1827 by the architect John Nash, who transformed a straight canal into the undulating lake. In 1916, the lake disappeared when it was drained to make space for temporary government buildings. It was refilled in 1922.

On the east side of the lake stands the Swiss-chalet-style Duck Island Cottage, with its equally lovely little front garden, built by the Ornithological Society of London as a home for the park's birdkeeper. From here or from the Blue Bridge you have great views across the lake. Spotted the pelicans yet? If not, you can be sure to catch them being fed adjacent to the Duck Island Cottage between 2.30pm and 3pm.

Address The Mall, SW1A 2BJ, www.royalparks.org.uk/parks/st-jamess-park | Getting there Tube to Charing Cross (Bakerloo and Northern Lines) | Hours Daily 5am – midnight | Tip Visit the Churchill War Rooms, Churchill's original World War II bunker that tells the story of Churchill's life and legacy (www.iwm.org.uk/visits/churchill-war-rooms).

90_ St John Zachary Garden
The Goldsmiths' Garden

Not far from St Paul's, this small garden is surrounded by modern buildings and traffic flows past. Despite this location the space has a calm atmosphere and seems untouched by the hustle and bustle of the modern world. The Goldsmiths' Garden sits on the site of the former church and churchyard of the medieval church of St John Zachary, which was destroyed by the Great Fire of 1666. The garden was created in 1941 by fire-watchers and re-designed twice in later years. The upper part lies in the former churchyard with mature trees and some gravestones.

From here you can see the sunken garden on the site of the excavated church. The serene garden below and the traffic and hectic movement above present a peculiar picture, as if heaven and hell had swopped places. In the sunken garden a paved path leads around a rectangular lawn with a fountain at its centre. Benches sit against the retaining brick walls that are covered with climbers. Perennials grow at their feet, including columbines, fuchsias and Japanese anemones. The sculpture *Three Printers*, made in 1957 by Wilfred Dudeney, creates a focal point. The Portland Stone statue represents different aspects of newspaper-making: an editor, a printer and a newsboy.

One of the special characteristics of this garden is its close link to the history of London and its livery companies (or trade associations). The Worshipful Company of Goldsmiths has owned the land since the Middle Ages, and its first livery hall was built across the road in 1339. The Goldsmiths left their mark above the arched entrance in form of a leopard's head, the hallmark used to verify the purity of the silver. Other livery companies have left traces here as well: the Blacksmiths' Company commissioned the iron archway; the Constructors' Company installed the central fountain and the Company of Gardeners refurbished the garden in 1994–1995.

Address Gresham Street, EC2V 7HN, www.thegoldsmiths.co.uk | Getting there Tube to St Paul's (Central Line) | Hours Unrestricted | Tip The magnificent Goldsmiths' Hall (Foster Lane) holds several open days a year. Tours can be booked through the City Information Centre (+44 (0)20 7606 3030).

91 St Leonard's Church

'There's rosemary, that's for remembrance'

Just imagine visiting this church garden in Elizabethan times when Shakespeare very likely lived in Shoreditch, and the parish lay outside the city walls and consisted mostly of gardens and fields with some timber-framed buildings.

Despite its rural character, Shoreditch became a bohemian haunt because London's first two purpose-built theatres, the Theatre and the Curtain, were built here, as theatres were not allowed inside the city walls. The Theatre's proprietor, James Burbage, is buried in the churchyard as are his sons Cuthbert and Richard. Richard was a close friend of Shakespeare, and the first to play Romeo in *Romeo and Juliet*. Other celebrities of the time were followed suit and the church became known as 'the Actors' Church'.

A church has stood on the spot since Anglo-Saxon times. The original church was replaced by a Norman one, and when the medieval building fell into disrepair, a new, Palladian-style church designed by George Dance the Elder was built between 1736 and 1740. The churchyard was turned into a garden in the 19th century with paths, areas of lawn shrubs and flowerbeds. More recently, an unfortunate series of violent drug- and alcohol-related incidents took place here. Following its tradition to help homeless and addicted people to recover, the church worked together with the Spitalfields Crypt Trust to revive the garden. The New Hanbury Project, an initiative run by the trust to help rehabilitation, started to re-landscape the plot with fruit trees and raised vegetable and flower beds in 2015. Tree discs, inscribed with quotes from Shakespeare's plays and a mosaic depicting The Bard, forge the connection to the heyday of the church as a bohemian haunt for Elizabethans, and the fact that the church scenes for the television comedy *Rev* are filmed here is a link between old theatre and new. Locals and passersby love to sit in the garden and smell the rosemary.

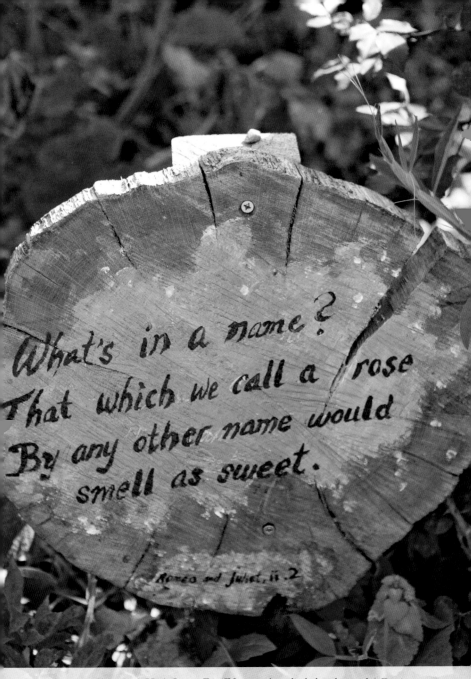

What's in a name?
That which we call a rose
By any other name would
smell as sweet.

Romeo and Juliet, II. 2

Address 119 Shoreditch High Street, E1 6JN, www.shoreditchchurch.org.uk | Getting there Tube to Old Street (Northern Line) or London Overground to Hoxton (East London Line) | **Hours** Unrestricted | **Tip** Have a coffee at Paper and Cup, a social enterprise coffee shop that also sells books and local artists' work (18 Calvert Avenue).

92 St Luke's Gardens

A break, with floral splendour

Are you shopping on the King's Road? If you would welcome a little time off to sit and relax, St Luke's Gardens is just the place for you. This quiet 2.5-acre park is only a few minutes from the famous shopping street and provides a lovely surprise for anyone who is daring enough to venture away from the King's Road.

The garden is overlooked by the handsome Grade I listed St Luke's Church, the first neo-Gothic church in London, built between 1820 and 1824 by James Savage. It was designed to accommodate 2,500 people and the 60-foot-high nave is the tallest of any parish church in London. On 2 April, 1836 Charles Dickens married Catherine Hogarth here, as did the parents of Robert Baden-Powell, the founder of the Scouting movement.

St Luke's surrounding graveyard was closed to burials in 1857, and it became a public garden in 1881. The gravestones were removed and now form the boundary wall. James Veitch, a local plant collector and nursery owner, was commissioned to do the planting to the design of the Borough surveyor, Mr. Strachan. The Countess Cadogan, a patroness of the church, opened the garden.

The paths form a curved cross. A separate area to the north of the church contains a children's playground and two multi-use game areas. The garden to the south features formal borders, some with a central palm tree and elaborate seasonal planting displays of tulips, hyacinths, daisies and primroses in spring. Numerous benches invite residents and visitors to take a seat and admire the floral splendour. The circular rose beds come into their own in early summer. The hawthorn and blackthorn planted near the perimeter buzz with the insects they were planted to attract. Mature trees such as tree of heaven (*Ailanthus altissima*), weeping ash (*Fraxinus excelsior pendula*) and chestnut trees give shade to the tired shopper. Are you still keen to continue your shopping?

Address Sydney Street, SW3 3UD, www.rbkc.gov.uk/leisure-and-culture/parks/st-lukes-gardens | Getting there Tube to South Kensington (Circle, District and Piccadilly Lines) | Hours Daily 7.30am–dusk | Tip Cabbages & Roses (123 Sidney Street) sells homeware, fabrics and fashion with traditional English flower patterns.

93 __ St Mary Aldermanbury

The lost Wren church

The garden and former churchyard of St Mary Aldermanbury, one of the 'lost Wren churches', is beautifully laid out but there are some aspects the visitor will find puzzling.

A church was first erected on the site around 1181. The churchyard was in use from 1250 and the church was extended in 1438. The Great Fire of London destroyed St Mary Aldermanbury in 1666 as it did so many other churches (88 including St Paul's) and it was rebuilt by Christopher Wren in 1671–75. The building was badly damaged by a bomb in World War II.

Today the footprint of the medieval church can still be seen in the garden but there is no trace of the church. Where did it go? A plaque solves the mystery: Wren's St Mary Aldermanbury now stands proudly in Fulton, Missouri, USA. It was dismantled in 1964 and re-erected at Westminster College in Fulton, where Winston Churchill was awarded an honorary degree and held his famous 'Iron Curtain' speech. The church was rebuilt as a memorial to the prime minister and houses the National Churchill Museum.

The London churchyard was purchased by the City of London in 1970 and laid out as a public garden. Today it features an ornamental box hedge knot garden, beds planted with flowers and shrubs, raised seating areas, mature trees and a lawn with the remnants of Old St Mary Aldermanbury. But wait, there's also a plinth topped with a bust of William Shakespeare. What is he doing here, in a part of the city where he never lived or worked? The inscription on the plinth solves this second puzzle. Charles Clement Walker of Shropshire donated this monument to the nation in 1896 in memory of John Heminge and Henry Condell, two of Shakespeare's fellow actors, who lived in the area and collected and published his works. So the church wasn't lost after all, and the garden does a pretty good job telling the story of St Mary Aldermanbury, and more.

Address Love Lane, EC2 2V, www.cityoflondon.gov.uk | Getting there Tube to St Paul's (Central Line) | Hours Unrestricted | Tip Guildhall (Gresham Street) has been the centre of London's government since the Middle Ages. Visit the Guildhall Art Gallery with a Roman amphitheatre underneath (www.guildhall.cityoflondon.gov.uk).

94__St Mary Magdalene Gardens

A garden for Holloway Road

Holloway Road is one of the major arteries channelling traffic into North London. There are many cars and few trees, and most people here are in a rush to get to their destination. But passers-by often slow down or stop when they reach the low wall separating this garden from the pavement. They breathe more deeply, look up into the large trees or try to get a sniff of the roses.

The church St Mary Magdalene (today called Hope Church), surrounded by its 4.5 acres of garden, began life as a chapel of ease for Islington parish church, meaning that around 200 years ago the parish population had grown so much that an additional church was needed. The neoclassical chapel was erected for the sum of £30,000. Following an Act of Parliament the surrounding churchyard was converted from a burial ground into a public garden in 1894. Many of the headstones were removed – some can still be seen near the church – and formal rose beds were added.

Since then, the garden has been a hub for the local community and the church offers meeting space for diverse associations. Families come here with packed lunches; schoolchildren play hide and seek; joggers and dog walkers circulate. When the pavement of Holloway Road is steaming with heat, the ash, lime and 39 mature plane trees provide shady spots that encourage sitting down for a moment, reading a book or just dreaming. One of the trees was even planted in the 18th century.

In 2010 the garden was refurbished with new lighting, plantings, seating, nest boxes and bird feeders. A beautiful perennial border near the road glows with *Rudbeckia* and *Verbena bonariensis* in late summer. It frames the view of the church and invites the visitor to come on inside.

Address Holloway Road, N7 8LT, www.stmarymagdalenegardens.org.uk | **Getting there** Tube to Highbury & Islington (Victoria Line) | **Hours** Daily 8am–dusk | **Tip** If you are interested in vintage shop fittings, visit characterful D&A Binder on 101 Holloway Road (www.dandabinder.co.uk).

95 St Mary's Secret Garden

Gardening for health

This small community garden has a special mission. Based on findings from doctors, physiotherapists and occupational therapists, who use gardening in therapy, St Mary's Secret Garden took up the cause of promoting well-being by gardening. The community garden, named after St Mary's Church Haggerston, has been a horticultural therapy project since 1997, but got its current name and status as a community garden in 2003. The organisation collaborates with GP practices and social service coordinators, working with HIV patients and people with cognitive impairments, and offering courses for people with learning disabilities and therapeutic placements for individuals with disabilities and long-term health problems. Also part of the programme are gardening tours for schoolchildren. Volunteers not only maintain the garden but also work closely with clients and support them.

You'll find traces of this work and community spirit everywhere in the garden. You can see people re-potting, watering, planting or harvesting. Every container or vessel here – from old shopping trolleys and bathtubs to tyres – overflows with plants. So many different habitats are packed into less than an acre. There is a woodland garden with working beehives; wild areas encourage butterflies, bees, moths and ladybirds; beautiful smells emanate from a herb and sensory area. Fruits and vegetables are grown in raised beds, and colourful wooden signposts spell out poems and plant names. A small pond, a herbaceous border and the Wish you Well Garden with a raised area for events complete the garden.

Before you leave, consider supporting the garden by buying some plants, bulbs, seeds or delicious jams and chutneys. They are all grown, harvested and made here by clients, learners and volunteers using organic methods. Other ways to support gardening for health are listed on their website.

THE HERBS

MOTHER NATURE'S M

COLOSSAL BAY TREE

ER OF THEM ALL

ROTECTING THEM F OM

LIKE THE HARD RAIN

THE FLY NG TH

Address 50 Pearson Street, E2 8EL, www.stmaryssecretgarden.org.uk, info@stmarysgarden.org.uk | Getting there London Overground to Hoxton (East London Line) | Hours Mon–Fri 9am–5pm | Tip Swedish bakery Fabrique produces good sourdough bread and other Swedish baked goods (Arch 385, Geffrye Street).

IS THE S EPHE D,

96__ St Pancras Gardens
Growing history

Most passers-by rush past a small garden on Pancras Road near St Pancras International Station, but anyone who takes the time to climb the steps to St Pancras Old Church and Gardens will be rewarded. The church was erected in the 11th or 12th century with a major rebuild in the 19th century. Its origins as a site of Christian worship are however much older, dating back to the 4th century. During the French Revolution the churchyard was used to bury Roman Catholics and refugees. In 1855 it had to give way to the expanding railway system and was partly destroyed, causing a public outcry. Thomas Hardy, the famous author and poet, was then studying architecture and had to supervise the removal of gravestones and bodies. An ash tree surrounded by gravestones that have fused with the wood over time is today called The Hardy Tree.

The burial ground was subsequently turned into a public park, one of the first of its kind. It is laid out geometrically with a tall memorial sundial in its centre. Donated in 1879 by Baroness Burdett-Coutts, a benefactress and one of the richest women in Britain, the monument is enclosed by a balustrade featuring statues of dogs in each corner – said to be modelled on Burdett-Coutts' own dog. Another important monument is the Soane Mausoleum, designed by the famous architect himself, where Soane, his wife and his son are interred. Its architecture inspired Sir Giles Gilbert Scott's design of the iconic K2 telephone box. Mary Wollstonecraft, who wrote *The Vindication of the Rights of Women,* has a tomb here, as does her daughter, *Frankenstein* author Mary Shelley, who allegedly had her first romantic rendezvous with future husband Percy Bysshe Shelley next to her mother's grave. Many more stories prove that St Pancras Gardens is steeped in London history, and, in the case of The Hardy Tree, it literally grows through it!

Address Pancras Road, NW1 1UL, www.camden.gov.uk | Getting there Tube to King's Cross (Northern, Metropolitan, Hammersmith & City, Circle, Victoria and Piccadilly Lines) | Hours Daily 7am–dusk | Tip Relic Antique Warehouse stocks quirky antiques and folk art (133–135 Pancras Road).

97__Stephens House and Gardens

The uncrowned king of Finchley

Charles 'Inky' Stephens acquired this Italianate villa and grounds in 1874, when it was Avenue House. The house had been built for the Reverend Edward Philip Cooper in 1859 but the history of the grounds goes back to 1243, when the Knights Templar were granted a plot of 40 acres here called Temple Croft Field.

Stephens' family had lived in Finchley since 1844. His father, Henry Stephens, was the inventor of an indelible 'writing fluid' that wrote blue and dried black. The high quality inks accompanied Scott's South Pole exhibition and were used to sign the Treaty of Versailles. Charles took over the company after his father's early death. Besides being a businessman, he was also a chemist, a Conservative Member of Parliament, a philanthropist and a member of the temperance movement. Stephens' interest in water management shows in the garden, where he erected a water tower. He also installed a water harvesting and irrigation system, which were reintroduced in 2016–17 to feed the bog garden, cascade and pond.

Stephens commissioned Robert Marnock to landscape the garden, which included lawns, ponds, a rockery and a kitchen garden called The Bothy Gardens with walls on three sides, topped by corner towers, which today contains a wild garden with unusual plants and a formal garden with a pergola draped in roses.

The garden also impresses with its fine collection of mature trees, including scots pine, fir, holly, oak, Caucasian wingnut (*Pterocarya fraxinifolia)* and a large Hungarian oak (*Quercus frainetto)*. It is the favourite park of many Finchley locals to whom Stephens bequeathed the house and 10-acre garden. He wanted it to be 'open for the use and enjoyment always of the public under reasonable regulations', which earned him the moniker of the 'uncrowned king of Finchley'.

Address 17 East End Road, N3 3QE, www.stephenshouseandgardens.com | Getting there Tube to Finchley Central (Northern Line) | Hours Daily dawn–dusk, check website for more details | Tip After your visit, why not head north or south on the nearby Dollis Valley Greenwalk, which extends from Mill Hill to Hampstead Heath.

98__Tavistock Square
Shade-loving plants for Virginia

The fifth Duke of Bedford developed this square and named it after his eldest son. It was built first by James Burton from 1803 and completed in the early 1820s by Thomas Cubitt. The garden was laid out in 1825.

Charles Dickens lived at Tavistock House from 1851 to 1860, and wrote four of his novels here. Now that corner is occupied by the Medical Association headquarters. Sadly it was just outside this building that a double decker bus exploded and 13 people were killed by a suicide bomber in 2005.

There is hardly a square in Bloomsbury without a connection to Virginia Woolf, and Tavistock Square is no exception. She lived from 1924 to 1939 at 52 Tavistock Square together with her husband, Leonard Woolf. Several of her novels were written here and she was even inspired to write *To the Lighthouse* when walking around the square. The Woolfs' house was also the first home of Hogarth Press, the publishing company run by Leonard Woolf. Virginia's bust in the garden, erected by the Virginia Woolf Society, is a copy of a bust sculpted by Stephen Tomlin in 1931. Leonard Woolf has a ginkgo biloba tree dedicated to his memory.

The centrepiece of the garden is a statue by Fredda Brilliant depicting Mahatma Gandhi, the great Indian civil rights leader, who studied at London University. A bronze bust portrays Louisa Aldrich-Blake (1865–1925), one of the first female British surgeons. Close to the North Gate a flowering cherry tree reminds visitors of the victims of Hiroshima.

The garden was restored and re-opened in 2011. The new planting includes four flower beds relating to the park's memorials. Ghandi's features plants from India; native Japanese plants were planted next to the Hiroshima Tree; Aldrich-Blake's herbal bed relates to her medical profession and Virginia Woolf got shade-loving English plants.

Address Tavistock Square, WC1H 9EZ, www.friendsoftavistocksquare.org.uk | **Getting there** Tube to Russell Square (Piccadilly Line) | **Hours** Daily 7.30am–sunset | **Tip** Thirsty? Like the taste of apple? Try Euston Tap, a bar dedicated to cider at 190 Euston Road.

99 __ Thames Barrier Park
Keeping it simple

This park is named after the imposing 520-metre-long flood barrier that spans the Thames near Woolwich. The world's second largest moveable flood barrier creates a dramatic backdrop for the thoroughly modern garden, which is framed on two sides by housing blocks.

The 22-acre plot is mostly grassland divided vertically by strips of trees such as birch and pine tree, and is cut horizontally in two by the Green Dock, a sunken garden with five-metre-high irrigated green walls of evergreen honeysuckle (*Lonicera pileata)*. A steel bridge connects the two upper parts of this garden; inside, tall undulating yew hedges run in waves towards the Thames. Between them geraniums, grasses and other perennials provide colour in the summer. At the end of the sunken garden an open pavilion on slender steel columns hardly obstructs the view of the glittering piers beyond. This Pavilion of Remembrance commemorates the victims of the London Blitz. There's also a café, a fountain, a children's play area and a basketball court in the park.

You can get another good view of the park and flood barrier from the DLR station. This view is probably most dramatic on a sunny winter's day, when the hedges aren't softened by flowering perennials. Standing in the same place 25 years ago you would have looked down on a brownfield site full of oil and tar, polluted by chemical and dye works, an armaments factory and a tarmac plant. Thankfully, in 1995 the London Docklands Development Corporation staged a competition to develop the site, which was won by Groupe Signes from Paris and Patel Taylor from London. They produced the first riverside park to be built in London for over 50 years.

Since its completion in March 2000 it has won many landscape design prizes, with good reason. Even if you aren't a fan of minimalist garden design, you have to admit that here, 'keeping it simple' simply works!

Address North Woolwich Road, E16 2HP | Getting there Train to Pontoon Dock (Docklands Light Railway) | Hours Daily 7am – 7.15pm | Tip For old-fashioned afternoon tea dances walk to Brick Lane Music Hall on 443 North Woolwich Road (www.bricklanemusichall.co.uk).

100_Tibetan Peace Garden

A garden of contemplation

Right next to the Imperial War Museum in Lambeth is a small garden designed in deliberate contrast to the imposing 100-ton twin naval guns standing in front of the museum. The Tibetan Peace Garden was commissioned by the Tibet Foundation and opened by His Holiness the Dalai Lama in 1999. The circular garden was designed by the sculptor Hamish Horsley and is based on the Dharma wheel. At the centre of the circle a bronze cast of the Kalachakra Mandala, set in black Kilkenny limestone, symbolises world peace. Eight stone seats surrounding the mandala stand for the noble eightfold path in Buddhism: right view, thought, speech, action, livelihood, effort, mindfulness and concentration. On the north, south, east and west points of the garden, four contemporary Western sculptures represent earth, fire, air and water. The open area in between represents the fifth element, space. The planting consists of Himalayan and Tibetan herbs and shrubs, as well as jasmine, honeysuckle and scented roses that cover the pergola. The surrounding area is planted with birches and other trees.

As well as conveying Buddhist spirituality and culture, the garden also symbolises the need to create understanding between different cultures. It reminds visitors of the courage of the Tibetan people and their commitment to peace and non-violence. A tall pillar at the entrance to the garden is inscribed with a message from the Dalai Lama in different languages: 'Conflicts and mistrust have plagued the past century, which has brought immeasurable human suffering and environmental destruction. It is in the interests of all of us on this planet that we make a joint effort to turn the next century into an era of peace and harmony.'

This garden with its simple, harmonious design is a wonderful place to sit and think things through. As its name Samten Kyil indicates, The Tibetan Peace Garden is a true 'Garden of Contemplation'.

Address St George's Road, SE1 6ER, www.southwark.gov.uk/parks-and-open-spaces/parks/geraldine-mary-harmsworth-park | **Getting there** Tube to Elephant & Castle (Bakerloo and Northern Lines) | **Hours** Daily 7.30am–9.30pm | **Tip** A visit to the Imperial War Museum gives you much to contemplate.

101 __ Vauxhall City Farm
New pleasures

If you are in Central London and feel the urge to feed a goat, this is the place for you! You can also ride a horse or stroke alpacas that have starred in a *Star Wars* movie. Vauxhall City Farm began its life in 1976, when a group of architects squatting at St Oswald's Place founded the Jubilee City Farm (later changing the name). The farm shares its site with Vauxhall Pleasure Gardens, which undertook a major refurbishment in 2005, planting trees, building a new sports pitch, and, in collaboration with the City Farm, constructing paddocks for horse-riding.

Large black concrete columns mark the entrance to the park and are a reminder of the original Vauxhall Pleasure Gardens, which opened around 1660 and entertained visitors for over 200 years. Then called New Spring Gardens, they became popular in the 18th century, featuring several novelties such as the Turkish Tent and the Chinese Pavilion as well as ruins, arches, statues and a cascade. Events ranged from musical performances and fireworks to hot-air balloon ascents. Even the battle of Waterloo was re-enacted here in 1817. The gardens closed in 1859. A successor named Vauxhall Spring Gardens was opened in the 1970s and became a meeting point for the gay scene thriving in the surrounding bars and clubs. Sadly, the gardens became neglected and unsafe.

The re-development of the park and the City Farm gave new life to the site and made it a place for local people. At the farm children can book riding lessons or meet and feed pigs, rare-breed goats, horses, guinea pigs, ferrets, hedgehogs, turkeys, geese, budgies and of course the celebrity alpacas. It is also home to an ecology garden with a stag beetle nursery, bog and wormery. Fruit and vegetables are grown in the allotment plots. Visitors can also take part in spinning classes and cookery workshops. The farm may not be as glamorous as the former Pleasure Gardens, but it is equally entertaining.

Address 165 Tyers Street, SE11 5HS, www.vauxhallcityfarm.org | Getting there Tube to Vauxhall (Victoria Line) | Hours Tue–Sun 10.30am–4pm, closed over Christmas | Tip The recently restored Tea House Theatre combines high tea and poetry readings (www.teahousetheatre.co.uk).

102___ Vestry House Museum
'If any would not work neither should he eat'

Workhouse gardens were not for pleasure. The growing of crops such as onions, cabbages and potatoes and the rearing of livestock in a workhouse garden were undertaken to provide the workhouse with a cheap source of food. Surplus produce was sold to contribute to the running of the house. The garden offered employment for the inmates and improved their horticultural skills. The garden at Vestry House Museum in Walthamstow adheres to these principles – almost.

The building was erected by the vestry in 1730 to serve as a workhouse. A stone plaque above the entrance is inscribed with the above motto, making clear what was expected from the paupers who lived there, among them pregnant women and children. After 1840 the paupers were moved elsewhere and several different institutions occupied the house over the following decades, among them the police. In 1882 the Walthamstow Literary and Scientific Institute moved in, and later it became a private residence, until 1930, when the last owner offered the remainder of her lease to Walthamstow Borough Council, which opened a Museum of Local History and Antiquities on the premises.

What had once been the workhouse garden was turned into a display space for the museum. In 2001 the garden was restored to its original use. It now contains herbs, vegetables and dye plants that were listed in the vestry archives and typically grown in a workhouse garden. There's a row of beech trees running through where the garden was once divided in two. The raised beds are partly surrounded with clipped box hedging and a wild meadow area and flower bed attract insects and butterflies. Volunteers maintain the garden, and lots of great events, such as Apple Day, the Easter Egg Trail and poetry installations bring it to life.

Vestry House Garden is a workhouse garden with a slight difference – it is enjoyed by all who visit it.

Address Vestry Road, E17 9NH, www.vestryhousemuseum.org.uk | **Getting there** Tube to Walthamstow Central (Victoria Line) | **Hours** Wed–Sun 10am–5pm | **Tip** With highlights such as The Bremer Car, a Victorian parlour and a police cell, you shouldn't miss the museum, but if you want to go shopping, Walthamstow is home to the longest street market in Europe (Tue–Sat on Walthamstow High Street).

103 Victoria Embankment Gardens

A 'notable' walk

Promenading amidst these beautifully laid-out floral borders, try to imagine you're walking on massive sewers, because these gardens – long, narrow plots on the north side of the Thames between Black-friars Bridge and Westminster Bridge – were created following the embankment of the Thames from 1864. Chief Engineer Sir Joseph Bazalgette of the Metropolitan Board of Works proposed the undertaking in order to prevent sewage flowing directly into the river, finally realising an idea conceived by Sir Christopher Wren in 1666.

Alexander McKenzie designed the Main Garden over the sewers with a symmetrical bedding scheme and bandstand. Today the planting includes mature trees such as London planes and more exotic specimens like the manna ash (*Fraxinus ornus*) adjacent to the café, which is covered in scented white flowers in late spring. Mixed borders are planted with exotic foliage plants, perennials and annual bedding plants. The southwestern section was laid out by George Vulliamy and contains plane trees, trees of heaven (*Ailanthus altissima*), lime and Indian bean trees (*Catalpa bignonioides*). By day the gardens are very busy. Office workers eat their lunches; exhausted tourists nap on the lawns; parents and children play with the giant chess set. Most of them are not aware that there are other 'notable' presences in the park quietly watching all that's going on. Among their ranks are generals, composers, a Sunday school founder and a temperance campaigner. The philosopher and religious sceptic John Stuart Mill, the English bible translator William Tyndale and the Scottish poet Robert Burns look sternly down on the visitors. Around 20 statues and memorials are gathered in the gardens alone, and more can be seen on the river walk along the Thames. They are watching you!

Address Villiers Street, WC2N 6NS, myparks.westminster.gov.uk | Getting there
Tube to Embankment (Bakerloo, Circle, District and Northern Lines) | Hours Daily
7.30am – sunset | Tip For a bit of whimsy, look for the dolphin lamp posts and the
benches depicting winged sphinxes along the embankment.

104 Victoria Park

A pagoda for the East End

Opened in 1845, Victoria Park was the first public park in London. Queen Victoria commissioned the originally 190-acre space (today it has 213 acres) in response to the demand for green spaces in the East End. The architect and planner James Pennethorne, who also designed Kennington Park and Battersea Park (see ch. 7), began the transformation of brick fields, market gardens, gravel pits and farmland in 1842. The boot-shaped plot featured belts of trees around the perimeter, several lakes, formal borders and a Chinese pagoda. Modelled on a Chinese summerhouse, the pagoda originally stood in Hyde Park at the entrance of the Chinese Collection exhibition in 1842. It was subsequently sold to Victoria Park for £110 and placed on an island in the Western Lake. Pennethorne envisioned a Chinese bridge to join the island to the land, but ran out of money.

Swimming was always a popular pastime in the park. One of the lakes was used as a bathing pond, first open only to male swimmers. Later the lido was built (1936) but was demolished in 1990. Today no swimmers are allowed in the lakes, but numerous waterfowl such as herons, cormorants, swans, geese, moorhens and ducks enjoy them. Another prominent feature is the elaborate drinking fountain, donated by the philanthropist Angela Burdett-Coutts (see St Pancras Gardens, ch. 96), who, by the way, was disinherited by her family when, at age 67, she married her 29-year-old American secretary.

The use of the park as a platform for political meetings, rallies and speeches is a testament to its popularity among the East End inhabitants. A large grant from the National Lottery Fund fortunately made long-needed improvements to the park possible, which began in 2012. Among them was the reconstruction of the Chinese pagoda, destroyed in the 1950s, as well as the building of the Chinese bridge Pennethorne had always envisioned!

Address Grove Road, E3 5TB, www.towerhamlets.gov.uk | Getting there Tube to Mile End (Central, District and Hammersmith & City Lines) | Hours Daily 7am–dusk | Tip Check out the V&A Museum of Childhood (www.vam.ac.uk).

105_ Victoria Tower Gardens

Celebrating freedom

Officially opened in 1914, this triangular garden follows the embankment of the Thames and is bordered by the Houses of Parliament to the north and Lambeth Bridge to the south. There are a few herbaceous borders, mature trees and shrubs surrounding a central lawn. The newest addition is the Horseferry Playground, surrounded by metal railings with a River Thames theme. The outstanding features of the garden are several monuments celebrating freedom.

Auguste Rodin's *The Burghers of Calais* is a cast of the original sculpture Rodin made in 1889 for the town hall in Calais. It commemorates the 1347 event during the Hundred Years War when Edward III laid siege to Calais. Edward offered to spare the city if six of its leaders would give themselves up to him, wearing nooses around their necks, presumably to be executed. Rodin caught this moment of self-sacrifice in his sculpture. Fortunately the story doesn't end badly, because Queen Philippa persuaded her husband to spare the citizens as she thought their deaths would be a bad omen for their unborn child.

On the centre lawn the Buxton Memorial celebrates the emancipation of slaves in the British Empire in 1834. It remembers Thomas Fowell Buxton, who campaigned for abolition in Parliament, and was commissioned in 1865 by Buxton's son Charles and designed by Samuel Sanders Teulon.

The third monument to freedom here is the statue of Emmeline Pankhurst, the famous suffragette who campaigned for women's right to vote. Ironically, her statue by Arthur George Walker was unveiled in 1930 by Prime Minister Henry Baldwin, who opposed women's suffrage, and musicians from the Metropolitan Police, some of whom had arrested suffragettes, played at the ceremony. Now may be a good time to sit on one of the raised benches with fine views of the River Thames and think about what freedom means to you.

Address Millbank, SW1P 3JA, www.royalparks.org.uk/parks/victoria-tower-gardens, stjames@royalparks.gsi.gov.uk | Getting there Tube to Westminster (Circle, District and Jubilee Lines) | Hours Daily dawn–dusk | Tip For more food for thought on freedom and the vote, visit the adjacent Houses of Parliament on a guided tour or even attend a debate (www.parliament.uk).

106__ Wandle Trail

A hard-working river

The River Wandle is only about nine miles long but it has supported many industries. In the 17th and 18th centuries around 50 mills were working along the river, churning out flour, gunpowder, paper, iron, dyes, copper, snuff, leather, herbal oils, calico and silk. In Victorian times William Morris and Arthur Liberty had their workshops here.

Unfortunately its industrial heritage led to the river being one of the most polluted waterways in Britain. Sometimes the water was pink or blue from all the dyes and at one point it was so contaminated that it even caught fire. By the 1960s it was declared a sewer. Subsequent river clean-ups in the following decades were immensely helpful in slowly improving the water quality, and today it again supports a wealth of fish and other wildlife. Even the fascinating brown trout has been spotted here.

The Wandle Trail is a walking and cycling route that follows the River Wandle from Carshalton (the river is first visible at Wandle Park in Croydon followed by a culverted section) to Wandsworth, where it flows into the Thames. On its way it crosses more than ten parks and nature reserves as well as other attractions such as the Wandsworth Museum, Deen City Farm and the Wandle Industrial Museum in Mitcham, Surrey, where you can find out about the river's industrial past.

Look out for an array of birds too. The grey heron is very common along the river. Kingfishers can be seen if you sit long enough on the riverbank, as can Britain's tiniest bird, the goldcrest. Different species of dragonflies and damselflies hover over the water (in case you didn't know, dragonflies rest with their wings spread out, while damselflies fold their wings up). Many native British plants grow along the river, including beautiful bluebells in spring. Nowadays the River Wandle has more space to breathe and can hopefully work a bit less hard.

Address Starting point Croydon, CR0 4UP, www.merton.gov.uk/leisure/visiting/ attractions/wandletrail.htm | Getting there Train to Waddon (Thameslink, Southern) or Wandsworth Town (South West Trains) | Hours Unrestricted | Tip Merton Abbey Mills, where William Morris and Liberty had their workshops, features the last Wandle waterwheel in full working order. The wheelhouse is open for visitors at weekends (www.mertonabbeymills.org.uk).

107 __ Waterlow Park

A garden for the gardenless

Adjacent to Highgate Cemetery, Waterlow Park is one of the lesser-known green spaces in London, but visit it once and you'll come again! Here you'll find colourful perennial borders, a formal terraced garden, rockery, wildlife areas and picnic lawns, three ponds with a cascade fed by natural springs, a playground, tennis courts, a community kitchen garden and a 16th century manor house turned into an exhibition and event space complete with café. The existence of this park is due to former mayor of London Sir Sydney Waterlow (1822–1906). Waterlow bought several private estates, among them Lauderdale House, once inhabited by Charles II's mistress Nell Gwynne, and combined them to form a single park. He then gifted the 29-acre estate to the public in 1889 as a 'garden for the gardenless'. The philanthropist strongly believed that the creation of public parks was 'one of the best methods for improving the social and physical condition of the working classes.'

The park is a favourite Sunday haunt for young families who walk to the playground or watch waterfowl at the pond. Afterwards they head for lunch to the café in Lauderdale House where they can also attend various classes, take part in family events or visit antiques and craft fairs.

On the lawn in front of the house a sundial is engraved with the inscription: 'This dial plate is on a level with the top of the dome of St Paul's Cathedral.' Stairs lead down to the formal garden at the side, which features box parterres planted with a mix of annuals and perennials. Further down to the left is a path leading to the Park Centre with a lovingly planted rockery border. Imposing old trees can be found in several places, among them a hollow oak and a beautifully shaped yew tree.

Now it's time to sit on a bench next to Waterlow's bronze statue and admire his foresight, as well as the beautiful view over London!

Address Highgate Hill/Dartmouth Park Hill/Swains Lane, N6 5HG,
www.waterlowpark.org.uk | Getting there Tube to Archway (Northern Line) |
Hours Daily 7.30am–dusk | Tip After a walk in the park indulge yourself with
tea at High Tea of Highgate (www.highteaofhighgate.com).

108__Well Hall Pleasaunce

The borough's most popular rendezvous

Much less known than neighbouring Eltham Palace, this 13-acre garden is definitely worth a visit. It was opened in 1933 but the history of the park dates back to the 13th and 14th centuries, when a moated manor house (demolished in the 18th century in favour of Well Hall) stood on the site. Thomas More's son-in-law, William Roper, lived in the manor house from 1495 to 1577, and built the Tudor Barn, which remains in the grounds as a dining and function venue. Notable inhabitants of Well Hall included John Arnold, watchmaker to George III, and the children's author Edith Nesbit. After Nesbit and her husband left in 1922 the property became neglected and Well Hall was pulled down in the 1930s. The park was laid out with formal gardens, ponds and woodland, and a seat, sundial and plaque were erected in memory of the Labour councillor William Barefoot, a friend of Edith Nesbit, who supported the creation of the park.

The plot consists of interlinked formal gardens alternating with more loosely landscaped areas. The Italian Garden is long and narrow with a central lily pond, a circular sunken garden at one end and a wisteria-clad pergola at the other end. It was refurbished in 2002 when Italian cypress trees *(Cupressus sempervirens)* were planted and an exotic planting scheme was introduced in the sunken garden. The moat that surrounded the manor house features a 16th century bridge and nesting mallards and moorhens. In the walled garden four rose beds are arranged in a Tudor pattern. In the Woodland Glen you'll find many different species of trees including a strawberry tree *(Arbutus unedo)* and a maidenhair tree *(Gingko biloba)*. The ground was turned into a wildflower meadow where the flowers are allowed to seed. With all this and more to discover this garden is surely still 'the borough's most popular rendezvous' as the *Eltham Times* described it in 1936.

Address Well Hall Road, SE9 6SS, www.wellhall.org.uk | Getting there Train to Eltham
(Southeastern) | Hours Daily 8am–8pm | Tip The Bob Hope Theatre (Wythfield Road) is
an interesting community theatre with amateur performances.

109 __ West Norwood Cemetery
An unknown destination

With 40 acres of landscaped grounds and gently winding paths, over 60 Grade II listed monuments, a Greek Orthodox necropolis and probably the finest catacombs in London, West Norwood Cemetery (formerly South Metropolitan Cemetery) is worthy of being one of the 'magnificent seven'.

Opened in 1837 as the second of these, it was designed by William Tite, who used the Gothic style on all the buildings and created the cemetery in the garden style with the planting carried out by Buchanan and Oldroyd. The site had once been the ancient Great North Wood and a number of old oak trees were included in Tite's design, some of which date back to the 16th century. The catacombs created under the Anglican chapel had space for 2,000 coffins and a lift was constructed to lower the coffins from the chapel above. West Norwood also features the first crematorium, opened in 1915 in the former Nonconformist chapel. During World War II, the Anglican and the Nonconformist chapels were both damaged and later demolished. The catacombs were closed and two gardens of remembrance were created. Notable people laid to rest in the cemetery include Isabella Beaton, the famous cookery writer; Henry Tate, the sugar magnate and founder of the Tate Gallery; and the pottery manufacturer Henry Doulton, whose mausoleum is covered with red pottery tiles.

It is lovely to come here when carpets of spring flowers grow between the graves and memorials. They seem especially bright and abundant, reminding you that life doesn't stop, even in a cemetery. Old trees provide ideal habitats for many birds including owls and kestrels. This place also seems to be popular with West Norwood's cat population. Walking along the paths, you'll probably encounter one or two of them sunbathing on a gravestone or striding purposefully towards an unknown destination. Who knows? They might have an important appointment.

Address Norwood High Street, SE27 9JU, www.lambeth.gov.uk/places| Getting there
Train to West Norwood (Southern) | Hours Nov–Mar: Mon–Fri 8am–4pm,
Sat & Sun 10am–4pm; Apr to Oct: Mon–Fri 8am–6pm, Sat & Sun 10am–6pm |
Tip Are you interested in what's under the sea rather than underground? Amphibian
Sports is London's friendliest dive shop, and also offers diving courses (44a Chapel Road).

110_ World Peace Garden

If not now, when?

…is the motto of the World Peace Garden in Hampstead. Twenty years ago this was a piece of neglected wasteland. Thanks to the initiative of local estate agent Jonathan Bergman and the engagement of many local volunteers and patrons, the site has been transformed into an enchanted garden – a woodland glade that overlooks a London railway station!

The long, narrow plot dominated by large sycamore trees used to be a dumping ground for all sorts of rubbish. With the help of Michael Wardle (hard landscaping), Tony Panayiotou (planting and soft landscaping), consultants Andy Darragh and Simon Berry, as well as the hard work of many volunteers, a garden was created (despite difficult conditions – the plot stretches up a steep slope and many overgrown sycamore trees had to be removed) offering a delightful surprise to unsuspecting passers-by.

At the street entrance, glass Peace Tiles are inscribed with messages and images chosen by donors. Descending a flight of wooden steps the visitor follows the meandering wood-chip path to enjoy the sight of flowering magnolia trees, daffodils, tulips and camellias in spring. Logs and tree trunks support the terraced slopes and are used as seats and railings. In summer, roses, clematis and honeysuckle grow up the trees and ramble over woven arches. Children love the wishing well and the three small ponds that are lined with flag irises. There's a small stage at the bottom of the garden, where events and activities such as chess tournaments, yoga, storytelling and a toy-making day take place.

The busy railway station is always in sight and noises of trains arriving and departing can be heard from below. This provides the background music to the sound of the wind chimes and atmosphere of an enchanted woodland glade above. No doubt commuters some-times hear the chimes, look up and wish they could be here rather than there!

Address South Hill Park, NW3 2SB, www.worldpeacegardencamden.org, office@worldpeacegardencamden.org | Getting there London Overground to Hampstead Heath (North London Line) | Hours Mon–Sun 10am–6pm | Tip Visit the nearby former residence and museum of the romantic poet John Keats at 10 Keats Grove.

111 WWT London Wetland Centre

Birdwatcher's paradise

This is one of the few green spaces in London where winter is one of the best times to visit because several species of wild ducks such as wigean, teal, shoveller and pintail can be sighted at this time on the main lake. Overwintering birds descend in great numbers on the lakes and waterways. A favourite among birdwatchers is the rare and noisy bittern that prefers the denser reed.

You might have guessed that this open space is all about water. The London Wetland Centre is a unique nature reserve in South London, where over 100 acres of wetland play host to 180 different bird species.

The site, managed by the Wildfowl & Wetlands Trust, is one of nine Wetland Centres in the United Kingdom that were created to research and save wetlands. It opened to the public in 2000 and was created from the former Barn Elms reservoirs.

Winding paths lead through a flat landscape with watery meadows, lakes, marshes and lagoons. The landscape is beautiful if slightly melancholic in winter, but changes entirely in spring and summer. The meadows begin to flower with primroses, sweet violets, wild daffodils, coltsfoot and marsh marigolds and also the beautiful snake's head fritillaries. Among the many birds now are sand martins that nest here during the summer months in a sand bank created for them. The sustainable gardens such as the Slate Garden are an amazing sight in summer with seas of colourful perennials and grasses. You can listen to the reed-munching water voles, observe sunbathing lizards, grass snakes and of course many buzzing insects; and it is great to watch the resident otters play at any time of the year.

With six wildlife-watching hides, birdwatchers find themselves in paradise and even wildlife presenter Chris Packham counts the centre among his favourite places in the country.

Address Queen Elizabeth's Walk, SW13 9WT, www.wwt.org.uk/wetland-centres/london | Getting there Tube to Hammersmith (District & Circle Lines) then bus 33, 72 or 209 to Red Lion | Hours 1 Mar–31 Oct 9.30am–5.30pm; 1 Nov–28 Feb 9.30am–4.30pm | Tip Just across the river you'll find Craven Cottage, the iconic riverside football stadium of Fulham Football Club built in 1905 (www.fulhamfc.com).

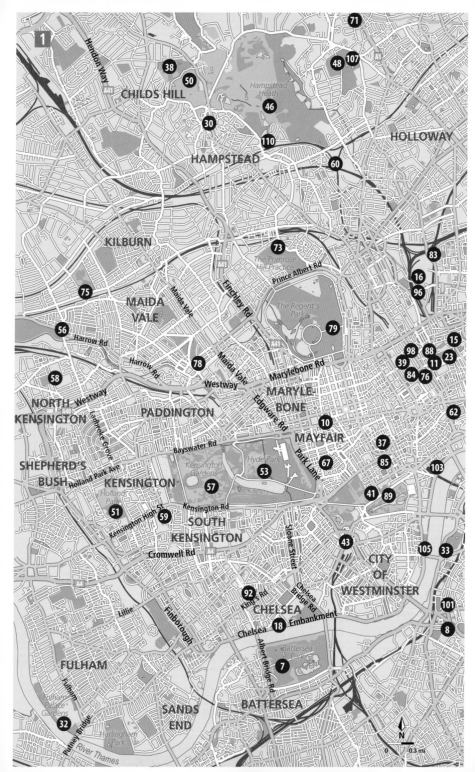

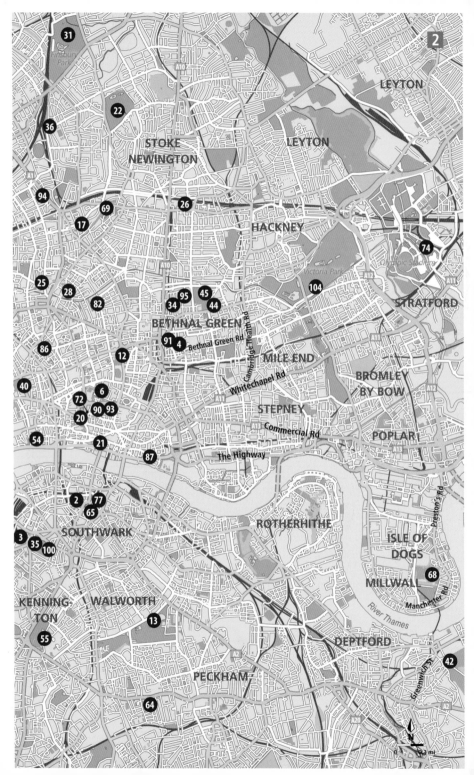

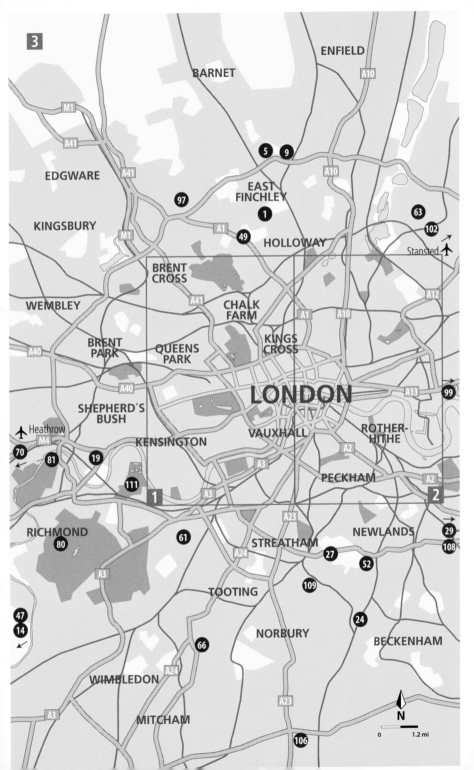

Lucia Jay von Seldeneck,
Carolin Huder, Verena Eidel
**111 PLACES IN BERLIN
THAT YOU SHOULDN'T MISS**
ISBN 978-3-95451-208-9

Rüdiger Liedtke
**111 PLACES IN MUNICH
THAT YOU SHOULDN'T MISS**
ISBN 978-3-95451-222-5

Rike Wolf
**111 PLACES IN HAMBURG
THAT YOU SHOULDN'T MISS**
ISBN 978-3-95451-234-8

Paul Kohl
**111 PLACES IN BERLIN
ON THE TRAIL OF THE NAZIS**
ISBN 978-3-95451-323-9

Sharon Fernandes
**111 PLACES IN NEW DELHI
THAT YOU MUST NOT MISS**
ISBN 978-3-95451-648-3

Sally Asher, Michael Murphy
**111 PLACES IN NEW ORLEANS
THAT YOU MUST NOT MISS**
ISBN 978-3-95451-645-2

Dirk Engelhardt
111 PLACES IN BARCELONA
THAT YOU MUST NOT MISS
ISBN 978-3-95451-353-6

Rüdiger Liedtke
111 PLACES ON MALLORCA
THAT YOU SHOULDN'T MISS
ISBN 978-3-95451-281-2

Peter Eickhoff
111 PLACES IN VIENNA
THAT YOU SHOULDN'T MISS
ISBN 978-3-95451-206-5

Frank McNally
111 PLACES IN DUBLIN
THAT YOU SHOULDN'T MISS
ISBN 978-3-95451-649-0

Gordon Streisand
111 PLACES IN MIAMI
AND THE KEYS
THAT YOU MUST NOT MISS
ISBN 978-3-95451-644-5

Marcus X. Schmid
111 PLACES IN ISTANBUL
THAT YOU MUST NOT MISS
ISBN 978-3-95451-423-6

Gerd Wolfgang Sievers
**111 PLACES IN VENICE
THAT YOU MUST NOT MISS**
ISBN 978-3-95451-460-1

Petra Sophia Zimmermann
**111 PLACES IN VERONA
AND LAKE GARDA THAT
YOU MUST NOT MISS**
ISBN 978-3-95451-611-7

Gillian Tait
**111 PLACES IN EDINBURGH
THAT YOU SHOULDN'T MISS**
ISBN 978-3-95451-883-8

Laurel Moglen, Julia Posey
**111 PLACES IN LOS ANGELES
THAT YOU SHOULDN'T MISS**
ISBN 978-3-95451-884-5

John Sykes
**111 PLACES IN LONDON
THAT YOU SHOULDN'T MISS**
ISBN 978-3-95451-346-8

Julian Treuherz, Peter de Figueiredo
**111 PLACES IN LIVERPOOL
THAT YOU SHOULDN'T MISS**
ISBN 978-3-95451-769-5

Annett Klingner
**111 PLACES IN ROME
THAT YOU MUST NOT MISS**
ISBN 978-3-95451-469-4

Kirstin von Glasow
**111 COFFEESHOPS IN
LONDON THAT YOU MUST
NOT MISS**
ISBN 978-3-95451-614-8

Giulia Castelli Gattinara, Mario Verin
**111 PLACES IN MILAN
THAT YOU MUST NOT MISS**
ISBN 978-3-95451-331-4

Rüdiger Liedtke, Laszlo Trankovits
**111 PLACES IN CAPE TOWN
THAT YOU MUST NOT MISS**
ISBN 978-3-95451-610-0

Jo-Anne Elikann
**111 PLACES IN NEW YORK
THAT YOU MUST NOT MISS**
ISBN 978-3-95451-052-8

Kathrin Bielfeldt, Raymond Wong,
Jürgen Bürger
**111 PLACES IN HONG KONG
THAT YOU SHOULDN'T MISS**
ISBN 978-3-95451-936-1